"Aphrodite T. Matsakis has once again captured the essence of the experience of individuals living with PTSD. This time, she has focused on helping those who love survivors understand the complexities and nuances of the issue. Matsakis has skillfully laid out key communication skills to utilize, as well as the common pitfalls to avoid in order to create trusting relationships. As a clinical social worker specializing in trauma therapy, I will recommend this book to the couples and individuals with whom I work. In addition, as a professor teaching graduate students, I know my students will benefit from Matsakis's expertise and techniques."

—**Eileen A. Dombo, PhD, LICSW,** clinical social worker, Washington, DC, and assistant professor at the National Catholic School of Social Service, The Catholic University of America

"For the past two decades, Aphrodite T. Matsakis has been helping people understand and cope with post-traumatic difficulties. In her latest book, *Loving Someone with PTSD*, she turns her focus to the survivor's relationship with the intimate partner. As always, Matsakis's advice is rock solid, down-to-earth, and immediately applicable. Bolstered by thought-provoking questionnaires and exercises, she guides the reader to create a safer, more authentic relationship that will sustain both survivor and loved one. This book will benefit everyone who cares about someone who has been touched by trauma."

—**Don R. Catherall, PhD,** professor of clinical psychiatry and behavioral sciences, Feinberg School of Medicine, Northwestern University, and author of *Emotional Safety*

"Those who love and care for PTSD sufferers feel ignored and mistreated. The caregivers often suffer silently, not knowing what to think or what to do. Aphrodite T. Matsakis has done a magnificent job describing a loved one's distress when trying to help and cope with a partner's PTSD. The author covers issues such as the feeling of helplessness, not only in the PTSD survivors, but in the comforters. Matsakis explains PTSD symptoms, how difficult it is to communicate with a PTSD sufferer, and psychological triggers that may drive a survivor into a rage. She also shows readers how to cope with a survivor's panic attacks, addictions, suicidal thinking, alcoholism, and drug addiction. She describes common therapies and lists the right questions to ask a person in pain and in despair. *Loving Someone with PTSD* is a stunning achievement, a beautifully written book that flows from the heart with simplicity and clarity. It will not only save relationships—it will save lives."

—**Allen R. Kates, MFAW, BCECR,** author *CopShock: Surviving Posttraumatic Stress Disorder (PTSD)*

"A helpful guide for people seeking practical advice when their relationship is falling apart under the stress of trauma. Survivors and those who love and care for them will discover new ways to strengthen and deepen their relationships and reverse the destructive effects of posttraumatic stress."

—**Stephen Joseph, PhD,** author of *What Doesn't Kill Us: The New Psychology of Posttraumatic Growth*

loving someone
with
PTSD

A Practical Guide to
Understanding and Connecting
with Your Partner after Trauma

APHRODITE T. MATSAKIS, PhD

New Harbinger Publications, Inc.

Publisher's Note

Distributed in Canada by Raincoast Books

Copyright © 2013 by Aphrodite Matsakis
New Harbinger Publications, Inc.
5674 Shattuck Avenue
Oakland, CA 94609
www.newharbinger.com

Cover design by Amy Shoup; Text design by Michele Waters-Kermes; Acquired by Melissa Kirk; Edited by Susan LaCroix

Library of Congress Cataloging-in-Publication Data

Matsakis, Aphrodite.
  Loving someone with PTSD : a practical guide to understanding and connecting with your partner after trauma / Aphrodite T. Matsakis.
      pages cm. -- (The New Harbinger loving someone series)
  Summary: "There are many books written for those suffering from post-traumatic stress disorder (PTSD), but few written for the people who love them. In Loving Someone with PTSD, a renowned trauma expert and author of I Can't Get Over It! presents concrete skills and strategies for the partners of those with PTSD. Readers will increase their understanding of the signs and symptoms of PTSD, improve their communication skills with their loved ones, set realistic expectations, and work to create a healthy environment for both their loved one and themselves. In addition, they will learn to manage their own grief, helplessness, and fear regarding their partner's condition"-- Provided by publisher.
  Includes bibliographical references.
  ISBN 978-1-60882-786-2 (pbk.) -- ISBN 978-1-60882-787-9 (pdf e-book) -- ISBN 978-1-60882-788-6 (epub) 1. Post-traumatic stress disorder. 2. Post-traumatic stress disorder--Patients--Family relationships. 3. Couples--Psychology. I. Title.
  RC552.P67M366 2014
  616.85'21--dc23
                                          2013039163

FSC
www.fsc.org
MIX
Paper from responsible sources
FSC® C011935

RAINFOREST ALLIANCE CERTIFIED

Printed in the United States of America

15   14   13

10   9   8   7   6   5   4   3   2   1   First printing

Dedication

"The world breaks every one and afterward many are strong at the broken places," wrote Ernest Hemingway. This book is dedicated to all who have suffered, directly or indirectly, as the result of human cruelty, human error, or tragic events beyond their control.

Contents

Acknowledgments   vii

Introduction   1

1   What Is PTSD?   15

2   PTSD and Your Relationship   39

3   Basic Communication Skills   49

4   Talking About Difficult Subjects and Making Decisions Together   93

5   Managing Triggers and Trigger Reactions   123

6   Crises: Panic Attacks, Rage Reactions, Domestic Violence, Addiction, and Suicide   159

7   PTSD Therapy and You   199

Helpful Resources   223

References   237

Acknowledgments

I'm grateful for the creative labors of Melissa Kirk, Nicola Skidmore, Jess Beebe, and the other New Harbinger staff who contributed their ideas and support, and for the work of copyeditor Susan LaCroix.

I owe a special debt of gratitude to my therapy clients—the many veterans, abused people, accident and torture victims, and other trauma survivors and their family members who had the courage to be honest about their struggles and share them with me. Without them, this book would not have been possible.

These men and women have served as models of inspiration in their efforts to build a strong relationship in the midst of what, for most people, would be unbearable emotional stress. I'm also deeply indebted to the many people in my family who taught me the meaning of persevering under adversity and the importance of family ties.

Introduction

Love matters. The ability to give and receive love is one of life's chief joys and sources of satisfaction. Without love, even major successes can eventually come to feel empty and dry.

Caring relationships help us cope with our fears and the hassles of everyday life and give us the support we need during times of trouble. People who have a strong relationship with a mate have been found to weather the storms of life better than those who feel unloved. They've also been found to have stronger immune systems and live longer (Johnson 2002).

Your Love Is Important

The support provided by others, especially a mate, helps soothe the feelings of loss, despair, and helplessness experienced by people who suffer from post-traumatic stress disorder (PTSD) due to combat, police work, natural catastrophes, physical or sexual assault, or another trauma. According to trauma experts, the single most important factor contributing to a person's recovery from trauma is the ability to receive comfort and love from another human being (van der Kolk et al. 1996).

If your partner suffers from PTSD, your love can play a major role in his healing. You can't be his therapist. But your ability to respond constructively to his symptoms and the challenges they bring to your relationship can make an important difference, not only in terms of his recovery, but in terms of your happiness and well-being too.

The purpose of this book to help you find ways of being supportive of your partner and coping with your PTSD-related relationship problems that take into account not only your partner's PTSD, but your needs as well.

The Recovery Environment

By learning about PTSD and developing certain coping skills, you'll be doing your part to improve your relationship and limit the damage caused by your loved one's trauma. But your partner must also make an effort. And there needs to be a recovery environment that supports his efforts.

Your sensitivity to his PTSD is critical. But his healing will also depend on many other factors—for example, how much support he receives from other family members, friends, and the general community; the availability of quality health care and other services; and the number and severity of the traumas he experienced. In general, exposure to one traumatic experience requires less recovery time than exposure to a series of traumas.

Recovery time is also influenced by the financial, emotional, and medical consequences of the trauma and by the number and nature of any especially positive or negative events that occurred after the trauma. For example, the returning soldier who can't find a job, who loses several family members in a car accident, or whose home is destroyed by a flood will probably have more adjustment problems than one whose return isn't strained by major losses.

Social prejudices based on age, gender, ethnicity, sexual orientation, or religion can also make recovery harder and longer. The same holds true for survivors who struggle with both an addiction and PTSD, who had medical or psychiatric problems before their trauma, or who have one or more family members experiencing a major stress or life change.

All PTSD cases are not the same. Symptoms vary in degree and form from one person to the next, depending on the individual's personality, religious or spiritual beliefs, culture, and thoughts about the meaning of the trauma. For example, Don, who lost his home in a fire, viewed the fire as a punishment for not having paid his ex-wife child support. Hence Don needed more therapy than his roommates, who didn't blame themselves for the fire.

You Are Not Alone

Not everyone who is traumatized develops PTSD. Some develop other psychiatric disorders, such as clinical depression. And others suffer only temporary or relatively minor symptoms that never develop into PTSD or any other official psychiatric disorder (though sometimes symptoms emerge years later, following another trauma or major loss). For the purposes of this book, however, the term "survivor" will refer to those survivors with PTSD.

As of the writing of this book, the lifetime prevalence of PTSD among adult Americans is estimated to be approximately 6.8 percent, or some 17 million people (Gradus 2011). This figure, however, doesn't include the many people whose PTSD is masked by an addiction or who don't seek help (and hence can't be counted). It also doesn't include the many people who have enough PTSD symptoms to cause problems, but not enough to be diagnosed with full-blown PTSD.

PTSD and Relationships

Although PTSD sufferers are troubled by their symptoms, they're usually far more distressed by the ways their symptoms and traumatic memories interfere with their ability to function in the present. PTSD damages the ability to pursue a career in some survivors more than others; however, almost all survivors have relationship problems.

Trauma can damage one's ability to trust, not only other people, but also oneself. Yet without some basic sense of trust and faith in oneself and in others, relationships—especially intimate ones—are hard to establish and maintain. The more betrayals a survivor experienced, the more difficulty he may have trusting and being close to others.

On the other hand, there are also survivors, especially among those who were abused as young children, who maintain a childlike faith in the goodness of all humankind. Therefore they can easily be manipulated by others. There are also survivors who alternate between being extremely cynical and extremely naive. Still others have been so beaten down by life that they are quick to trust almost anyone who offers help or support, without checking out the sincerity or credentials of that person (or organization).

Some survivors can be wary of most people, yet blinded by compassion toward fellow survivors or others who suffer—or who pretend to suffer, or exaggerate their sufferings, in order to take advantage of the survivor. Some survivors overidentify with other survivors, not realizing that even if someone was traumatized or suffers in a similar way, it doesn't necessarily mean that person is honest. Being either overly suspicious or overly trusting can create problems with a partner who is able to judge the sincerity of others more realistically.

As is well known by now, when one person in a family suffers, other family members suffer too. If you love someone with PTSD, you can't help but be affected by his mood swings or his seemingly unpredictable reactions to others—especially to you, his partner and mate.

At times it may seem as if you're the most important person in his life. Indeed, you may be the one to whom he turns when his anxiety and sadness feel unbearable or when he feels frightened and confused by his flashbacks and nightmares. Perhaps he's even stated that you're his main reason for living, or that without you by his side he'd have given up long ago. Yet at other times, you may be the target of his frustrations with himself, his despair about the future, or his anger at those who he feels acted unjustly during his trauma.

Other times he may withdraw from you altogether and seem surrounded by a wall that shuts you out. During those times, whether you ignore him, try your best to please him, or even try to pick a fight with him, you can't pierce his wall. You may then feel alone, abandoned, and quite unappreciated.

You may also feel resentful, yet wonder if you have the right to feel resentful. "My partner wouldn't be having all these problems if he weren't traumatized," you may reason. Yet sometimes you may also wonder if he's using PTSD as an excuse.

Respecting Your Own Pain

Your partner has sadness and pain born from his horrible experiences. But you have a different kind of sadness and pain. Yours is the sorrow of loving and wanting more closeness with someone you don't always understand or know how to react to—or whether to react to at all.

Sometimes he's so loving toward you and seems so dependent on your love. But other times he won't let you love him at all. Meanwhile, some of your deepest needs go unmet. Your suffering is real, just as real as your partner's. There is no hierarchy of grief, where only those with certain kinds of pain are entitled to feel sad.

Do you feel you're shouldering more financial and other responsibilities than you'd like to, or ever expected to, because of his PTSD? Having to do more than you're willing or able to do can create additional stress for you and your relationship.

There Is Hope

Unfortunately the media often portray PTSD sufferers either as walking time bombs capable of "going postal" and exploding at any moment or as homeless, pitiful creatures walking around in a daze. These damaging stereotypes of survivors as "crazy lunatics" or "hopeless cases" are false! PTSD is a condition that a person has; it is not the entire person. It's also a highly manageable condition. Like diabetes, with proper care and the right kind of support, PTSD symptoms can be controlled.

Some of your partner's memories and difficulties may remain forever. But the negative effects of his trauma can be considerably reduced. Today there are any number of effective therapies and other treatments for PTSD. They can't make his PTSD disappear. But they've enabled thousands of survivors to contribute to society and enjoy the benefits of an intimate relationship again.

Both the media and the mental health field tend to emphasize the negative effects of trauma. These negative effects are real. But recent research indicates that trauma can also develop various personal strengths and deepen relationships (Joseph 2011). Hence the turmoil you and your partner are experiencing may be laying the foundation for a stronger, more meaningful relationship. Just as you can't help but be affected by his problems, down the line you may benefit and be inspired by any emotional, spiritual, or other growth he might experience.

How This Book Can Help You: Book Overview

Whether your partner suffers from occasional bouts of PTSD symptoms or her PTSD is severe enough to have put her on disability, this book can provide you with some basic tools for helping not only her, but yourself. Despite the enormity of her pain and other problems, your life deserves attention and care too.

In chapter 1, "What Is PTSD?" you'll learn about PTSD and its possible effects on your moods, your partner's moods, and your ability to communicate with each other.

In chapter 2, "PTSD and Your Relationship," you'll take a close look at your original hopes for your relationship and how PTSD helped, or didn't help, your wishes come true. You'll then begin looking at the specific ways PTSD has affected both you as an individual and your relationship, and identifying some ways you'd like the relationship to improve.

Communication is a problem for many couples, especially couples in which one partner has PTSD. In chapter 3, "Basic Communication Skills," you'll identify some of the positive and negative ways you and your partner communicate, and then learn some positive communication skills to use with someone with PTSD.

In chapter 4, "Talking About Difficult Subjects and Making Decisions Together," you'll learn how you can affect a person's ability to make decisions and to discuss emotionally sensitive subjects, such as relationship issues. You'll then be shown ways to make your joint decision making go more smoothly, and to discuss relationship problems and other potentially explosive subjects in the most productive way possible. You'll also learn when and how to put certain topics on hold.

Like the rest of this book, chapters 3 and 4 don't promise a tension-free relationship. But by learning the skills and principles in these chapters, you'll increase your chances of being heard by your partner and of making progress toward your relationship goals.

In chapter 5, "Managing Triggers and Trigger Reactions," you'll learn more about triggers (reminders of one's trauma) and ways of helping your partner manage them. This chapter also provides suggestions for improving the safety of your living environment and for coping with long-standing triggers, medical appointments, social situations, and other types of triggers. Equally important, you'll be shown how to take better care of yourself when she's triggered.

Chapter 6, "Crises: Panic Attacks, Rage Reactions, Domestic Violence, Addiction, and Suicide," describes some of the causes of these crises and provides suggestions for coping with them until outside help becomes available.

Chapter 7, "PTSD Therapy and You," describes the different kinds of PTSD therapy currently available and how therapy can affect your relationship. It also provides suggestions for talking to your partner about trauma, for encouraging her to seek help, and for finding ways to better meet your own needs despite the pressing needs of your family.

"Helpful Resources" lists organizations, hotlines, books, and other sources of information and support for you and your partner.

This book provides some limited suggestions for coping with anxiety, numbing, and other problems. It isn't, however, a healing guide for depression, PTSD, or any other major psychiatric disorder. If you or someone in your family has a severe or ongoing form of emotional or mental distress, you'll also need to work with more specialized self-help books or with a licensed mental health professional. Legal help and other kinds of professional help are definitely necessary if you or someone in your household is being physically or sexually abused. (See the Resources section.)

If you're a trauma survivor too, parts of this book might bring to the surface painful aspects of your past. Hence you'll need to be especially careful to work with this book at your own pace and observe the cautions listed below.

Cautions

Treat yourself gently as you work with this book. Don't rush through it. When it comes to issues of the heart, there are no "fast fixes." All change, even positive change, is a process and takes time. Be as patient with yourself as you've been (or tried to be) with your partner.

Monitor yourself carefully so that you don't become emotionally overwhelmed or feel out of control in any way. It's normal to experience some upset in looking at certain aspects of your life. But if your distress doesn't decrease in a short time, or you begin having problems functioning, stop reading this book immediately. Then call your physician or a qualified mental health professional, or go to the emergency room of a local hospital.

Also stop reading this book and seek help if you experience any of the following: ongoing anxiety, depression, or numbing; suicidal or homicidal thoughts; increased desire to engage in substance abuse, self-mutilation, overspending, or some other self-destructive behavior; feeling out of touch with reality, even temporarily (for example, having hallucinations or especially vivid flashbacks); physical symptoms (such as bleeding, uncontrollable shaking, hyperventilation, extreme nausea, diarrhea, or any new or unexplained pain); or increased symptoms of a preexisting medical or psychiatric condition.

When the Suggestions in a Chapter May Be of Limited Use

If there's frequent verbal abuse in your relationship, especially if there's also physical violence, the suggestions in this book will be of limited use. For these suggestions to have any lasting impact, the person or people responsible for the abuse need to be in a treatment program specifically designed to stop the abuse.

Similarly, if your partner enjoys being cruel or has been diagnosed with antisocial personality disorder, the ideas in this book may have little effect. She needs to regularly attend intensive therapy aimed at helping her overcome her need to manipulate and mistreat others.

If she's abusive or cruel, however, she may be able to manipulate the therapist. She could also use going to therapy as a way of manipulating you. Hence her simply going to sessions is not enough. You need to see consistent signs of positive change.

The important word here is *consistent*. Most people can act better for a short time. But the changes need to be long-lasting before you can have some confidence that your partner is actually benefiting from counseling.

Writing and Reflecting: Keeping a Journal

Learning about PTSD and looking over some of the suggested coping skills in this book are good first steps toward improving your situation. But you'll get the most out of this book if, after reading each chapter, you spend ten or fifteen minutes writing about what you learned and how the material in the chapter affected and applies to you. Writing can help you release some of your feelings. It can also give you insight into the emotional truths of your life.

Some of these truths may be difficult to face. But only by facing them can you begin taking the necessary steps to lessen your stress and unhappiness. Writing can also help you uncover some of your inner strengths and positive aspects of your relationships that you hadn't fully appreciated before.

Questionnaires

Even if you already keep a personal diary, you'll need a separate notebook to record your thoughts and feelings as you read this book and to complete the questionnaires. These writing exercises are designed to help you find personal solutions to your PTSD-related relationship problems.

Write for yourself, not a professor. Don't worry about spelling or sentence structure. Let your thoughts flow freely in any language, or as many languages as you wish.

Feel free to change any specifics in the exercises to fit your experience. If a question refers to the survivor as female and your partner is male, substitute *he* for *she,* or vice versa. PTSD occurs among both men and women, of all sexual orientations. To reflect this reality, some parts of each chapter are addressed to readers with female partners and other parts, to readers with male partners.

You can skip around as you read this book and focus on those topics and exercises most relevant to you. Also feel free to skip over any sections that make you uncomfortable. It's essential that you read chapters 1 and 2, however, because they lay the foundation for the rest of the chapters.

Alternatives to Writing

If you don't want to use writing as a way of learning the material in this book and applying it to your specific circumstances, consider using meditation or some other kind of quiet reflection. Or maybe you think better when doing something active by yourself, such as swimming, gardening, or mindless chores. Whatever method you choose, set aside time to focus on the topics and exercises at hand someplace where you aren't distracted.

The Importance of Thinking Before Acting

In ancient Greek mythology, the goddess of wisdom, Athena (also the goddess of war), cautioned warriors to think before acting. She'd stop warriors from reacting impulsively or out of habit. Instead she advised them to study and assess not only the problem before them but also their own emotional and physical condition before deciding what to do.

But you don't have to be a warrior to benefit from this ancient wisdom. Since you've been with your partner, you've probably developed some ways of reacting to her that are almost automatic. Some of these habits may be helpful. But it's those that aren't that you'll be trying to change. Writing or reflecting on the material in this book and completing the exercises are ways of following through on the age-old advice to learn, observe, and assess before acting.

Indeed, one of the goals of PTSD therapy is to teach survivors to think before they act. Even a moment of thought can help them from reacting in ways that might have been reasonable during the trauma, but not so beneficial in the present.

A Final Note

This book is based on existing research on trauma and on more than thirty years of counseling survivors and their families. Although this book is written primarily for partners of survivors with PTSD, the well-being and needs of survivors are also considered.

In listening to the life stories of survivors and their partners and other family members, I've learned that there are no "good guys" or "bad guys." I've also learned that both the survivor and her partner often feel painfully different from other couples because they must cope with the effects of the past as well as the stresses of the present.

Yet the world is full of survivors and their families. Often, being in a partners' support group helps to lessen the feelings of isolation experienced by many partners. Hopefully this book can serve a similar purpose. And hopefully it will also remind you that you and your partner are not inferior (either individually or as a couple) simply because you've been wounded by tragic events that make it difficult for the two of you to connect at times.

As you read this book, you may find that particular sections or suggestions don't apply to your situation. That's because each individual and couple is unique. Also, the problems you and your partner face are influenced by many factors other than your individual personalities—for example, societal attitudes, finances, or physical injury. Due to space limitations, the topic of physical disability is not covered in this book. Yet even under ideal circumstances, such as excellent medical care and financial coverage, disability can be a nightmare for all involved.

This book is only a beginning guide toward improving your relationship and helping you take a closer look at your personal priorities. It is not intended to be, nor can it be, a substitute for medical and psychiatric diagnoses and treatment. You may need the assistance of qualified health professionals, and perhaps spiritual advisors, to help support your efforts.

CHAPTER 1

What Is PTSD?

This chapter explains how trauma can lead to PTSD, the symptoms of PTSD, and how your partner's PTSD might be affecting your relationship. It also provides guidelines for deciding when his symptoms are serious enough to seek help.

But PTSD is more than a checklist of symptoms. No psychiatric diagnosis can fully describe the degree of suffering experienced by survivors of war, family violence, a hurricane, or the suicide of a loved one. For many, the pain is not only emotional but physical, mental, and spiritual as well.

PTSD: A New Name for an Old Problem

The diagnosis of PTSD first appeared in 1980. But doctors, poets, and novelists have written about the effects of trauma throughout the ages. Perhaps the first documented case of PTSD is that of an uninjured Athenian soldier in 490 BCE. After witnessing his comrade's death, he developed a case of hysterical blindness (Herodotus 1890). Centuries later (during World War I) another soldier, Adolf Hitler, would also become temporarily blind during combat. Hitler was so humiliated by this experience that when he became dictator he banned the term "shell shock" and forbade giving psychiatric diagnoses to Nazi soldiers (Shepard 2003, Weber 2010).

Even high-ranking, highly trained people who are carefully screened before being assigned to dangerous duties can develop PTSD. And PTSD isn't limited to soldiers. It can develop among civilians of all ages and backgrounds, including those with no history of mental illness.

The Diagnostic Criteria for PTSD

According to the official definition of PTSD in the *Diagnostic and Statistical Manual of Mental Disorders* (*DSM-5*), to qualify as having PTSD, one must meet the following nine criteria (American Psychiatric Association 2013):

Criterion A: Exposure to one or more events involving actual or threatened death, serious injury, or sexual violence. The exposure can be either direct (experiencing the events or being physically present as the events happen to others) or indirect (finding out that a close friend or family member was violently victimized or seriously injured, or being repeatedly exposed to the details of horrifying events).

To qualify as a traumatic event, the actual or threatened death of a loved one must be violent or accidental. And indirect exposure to trauma from photos or the media doesn't count as traumatic unless the exposure is work-related.

Criterion B: Repeatedly reliving the trauma in the form of dreams, illusions, flashbacks, unwanted thoughts, or extreme emotional or physical reactions when confronted with reminders of the trauma. Reminders can be external (such as people, places, things, smells, sounds, tastes, or situations) or internal (such as emotions or physical sensations).

Criterion C: Avoiding (or making efforts to avoid) thoughts, feelings, or conversations about the trauma, or things that bring it to mind.

Criterion D: Trauma-related negative changes in thinking patterns, mental abilities, and mood, as evidenced by two or more of the following: highly pessimistic attitudes toward oneself, others, and the world; memory loss regarding important aspects of the trauma; blaming oneself or others for the trauma due to distorted beliefs about its causes and consequences; ongoing fear, anxiety, guilt, shame, anger, or other negative emotions; lack of interest in activities that were previously rewarding; alienation from others; problems feeling love, hope, satisfaction, or other positive emotions.

Criterion E: Noticeable changes in reactivity and arousal due to the trauma, as indicated by two or more of the following: irritability and angry verbal or physical outbursts (for little or no cause); sleep problems; reckless or self-harming actions; difficulty concentrating; constantly being on the lookout for danger (hypervigilance); sensitivity to unexpected sounds, sights, smells, or touch.

Criterion F: Symptoms in criteria B, C, D, and E last longer than a month.

Criterion G: Symptoms significantly interfere with the ability to work, relate to others, or pursue other important aspects of one's life.

Criterion H: The symptoms are not the result of medication, a medical problem, or substance use.

DISSOCIATIVE SUBTYPE

In addition to the PTSD symptoms listed above, some survivors also develop dissociative symptoms: feeling more like a thing than a person; feeling outside of—or detached from—one's body, thoughts, or emotions; or feeling as if one were in a dreamlike, distant, slow-motion, or distorted world.

DELAYED PTSD

Though PTSD symptoms can develop during the traumatic event, PTSD is by definition a delayed reaction. Typically, symptoms emerge soon after the trauma. Yet it is not unusual for symptoms to appear months, years, or even decades later. Full-blown PTSD emerging more than six months after a trauma is called "delayed PTSD."

Associated Symptoms

The following symptoms are also common among trauma survivors: panic attacks, depression, paranoia, suicidal thoughts, survivor guilt (guilt from having survived when others did not, or having been less injured than others), and many other kinds of guilt. For example, survivors often fault themselves for parts of the trauma over which they had little control, or for having violated a cherished personal standard in order to survive or help others survive (Kubany and Manke 1995). The resulting guilt lessens their ability to enjoy life, achieve success, or accept the love of others.

Some survivors also develop habits that seem strange but make perfect sense in light of their particular traumatic experiences. For example, an army nurse whose unit often lacked medical supplies learned to make bandages from bits of torn paper. To this day, when she throws away even the tiniest scrap of paper, she feels like she's killing a wounded soldier.

Variability Over Time

Having PTSD doesn't mean having symptoms every minute of every day. Symptoms can vary over time. For example, they tend to be more severe during anniversary dates of the trauma or times of personal, family, community, or national stress.

Symptoms can also lessen after a few years, then reemerge full force, and then lessen again. Over time, symptoms can also steadily decrease and become so occasional that they don't meet the criteria for PTSD. Yet even a few symptoms can affect one's life in undesirable ways.

Acute Stress Disorder

For some people, the effects of trauma are short-term. Typically, these people experienced a single traumatic event with few consequences other than temporary emotional shock. If their symptoms last no longer than three to thirty days, they are considered to be suffering from acute stress disorder.

Acute stress disorder can create some of the relationship problems described in this book. However, by learning helpful ways of coping with a loved one's acute stress disorder, a partner can help prevent these temporary problems from developing into longer-term ones.

Fight-Flight-Freeze (F-F-F) and Other Emergency Reactions

PTSD is listed as a psychiatric disorder. But it is basically a physiological one. The emotional and mental disturbances of PTSD stem from the physical changes that occur during trauma. Understanding the biological basis of PTSD is important. Otherwise you may view your partner's PTSD as a sign of weakness, an unwillingness to "let go of the past," or some inborn tendency toward being a "loner" or a "hothead."

In life-threatening (or potentially life-threatening) situations, our bodies release certain emergency stress hormones and biochemicals to help us survive. These alarm reactions help us either fight back with unusual strength (the fight reaction); run faster than we've ever run (the flight reaction); or stop short in our tracks (the freeze reaction). The freeze reaction gives us time to assess the danger and figure out a way to escape. If there is no means of escape, it helps us conserve our energy until one becomes available.

FIGHT-FLIGHT (F-F): ADRENALINE AND NORADRENALINE

Katy, a young mother, parked on an incline and forgot to put on her parking brake. By the time she began unbuckling her newborn in the backseat, her car was already rolling downhill toward a crowded intersection. Katy dashed to the back of the car and pushed against it. Even though the 100-pound Katy was recuperating from surgery, she managed to halt the vehicle's descent.

Katy's almost superhuman strength came from the massive amounts of adrenaline and noradrenaline released by her adrenal glands. (Noradrenaline is often used to help revive people experiencing heart failure or dangerously low blood pressure.)

Similar surges of adrenaline and noradrenaline empower soldiers to fight for long periods of time despite harsh physical conditions. The fight-flight response can also be seen in animals. For example, when Katy took her cat to the vet, it became so frightened that three trained assistants were needed to restrain it.

FREEZE RESPONSES: NATURE'S TRANQUILIZERS

Katy sprang into action when her child was in danger. Another parent, John, had a very different reaction. John's daughter was on their front lawn when a motorcyclist suddenly veered off the road and knocked her over. John wanted to rush to her side or call for help, but he couldn't move. Afterward he felt like a wimp and a terrible father. Yet his freeze response was totally involuntary.

Fear can put us into high gear in a matter of seconds. But it can also flood us with biochemicals that make us numb (van der Kolk, McFarlane, and Weisaeth 1996). The numbing can be physical, emotional, mental, or some of all three. For example, we may have difficulty speaking, moving, feeling, thinking, or remembering. Or we may develop feelings of unreality or other dissociative symptoms.

People in abusive relationships, prison camps, or other inescapable situations frequently experience some degree of mental and emotional numbing. They can't flee physically. But they can flee mentally by "spacing out," "forgetting," or screening out parts of their reality. This ability makes their lives more tolerable and helps them preserve some sense of control, self-respect, and personal identity.

Like mental numbing, emotional numbing provides a cushion between the person and the trauma. Without this buffer, soldiers, firefighters, police officers, and crime victims would have to experience the full impact of the horror, grief, and other intense emotions involved in their situation. The impact could easily interfere with their ability to do what is necessary to survive or complete their mission. Emotional numbing also protects people from uncontrollable shock, suicidal or homicidal feelings, and other potentially dangerous emotions.

Physical numbing blocks out pain. Hence it saves the sanity of those trapped underneath cars and helps the wounded walk for hours in search of help.

All Emergency Responses are Normal

Katy's frantic efforts to save her child and John's "shut-down" seem to be opposites. Yet they are part of the same phenomenon: the body's response to a perceived threat. Fight-flight-freeze reactions are all entirely normal and not a matter of will. They stem from the time when humans lived in the wild rather than in sheltered cities, and they're now hardwired into our anatomy.

In our society, however, fight-flight reactions tend to be viewed as heroic; freeze reactions, as shameful. Hence rape victims who fight back are praised. But those who go limp are either disbelieved or viewed with contempt.

In the past, soldiers who "froze" on the battlefield were usually considered traitors, cowards, or manipulators looking for a ticket home. They were punished accordingly. As late as World War I, hundreds of German, British, and French soldiers were executed as traitors or cowards because they couldn't stand up or speak, or displayed other signs of numbing (Shepard 2003).

It's not unusual for a person to have both fight-flight and freeze reactions during the same traumatic episode. This can be very confusing, especially to combat soldiers like Darnell, who was trained to be alert and in control of his reactions at all times. Once, Darnell walked for miles through enemy territory to reach his unit. Yet at one point he "blanked out." When he came to, he couldn't move. He still can't remember how long he ran or how long he lay in the mud, paralyzed. Darnell fought valiantly overseas. Yet his brief period of numbing is still a deep source of personal shame.

The Complexity of Alarm Reactions

The biology of PTSD is complex. During emergency situations the body releases not only adrenaline and noradrenaline, but numerous other biochemicals. Some of these substances can affect memory and emotional control. When stress is prolonged, the adrenal glands and some of these helping biochemicals can become depleted. This depletion can lead to depression, panic attacks, mood swings, rage reactions, and problems responding appropriately to others (van der Kolk, McFarlane, and Weisaeth 1996). (Due to space limitations, the many complexities and ongoing debates about the exact ways trauma affects the human body are not explained here.)

When Alarm Reactions Persist: The Origins of PTSD

Despite decades of research, there is no one theory that can explain the wide range of symptoms experienced by survivors. But all existing theories stem from one basic truth: that PTSD involves the continuation of F-F-F and other alarm reactions into present-day situations where there is no danger. Hence a person is victimized not only by an event, but by the memory of the event.

Suppose, for example, as a result of her experience with the rolling car, Katy couldn't drive without having a panic attack. This response would suggest that Katy might be suffering from PTSD, because reminders of her trauma (called triggers) consistently resulted in crippling alarm reactions when there was no cause for alarm.

The Domino Effect

Given that Katy's and John's brushes with death didn't result in severe injury, it's unlikely that they would develop PTSD. However if Katy had a history of trauma that she'd suppressed, the car incident could have triggered the onset of PTSD. Similarly, if John had worked in emergency services or a war zone for years without any apparent ill effects, the motorcycle incident might have been the proverbial "straw that broke the camel's back."

Some people can absorb several or a series of traumas without developing major symptoms. Yet there comes a point where the next trauma tips the balance, setting in motion what is often called the "domino effect." Here a single event can bring forth memories of prior traumas, leading to PTSD.

Emergency Responses, Mental Abilities, and Emotional Reactivity

Your partner's alarm reactions to nonthreatening reminders of his trauma can negatively affect his mental abilities and emotional control. Perhaps these things weren't as important when survival depended primarily on escaping from or overpowering wild animals or human attackers. But in modern times, survival also depends on memory and the ability to think logically and maintain complex social relationships.

It can be hard to understand why survivors have alarm reactions to reminders when the reminders, in themselves, aren't dangerous. But when a reminder is associated with the trauma, it signals to the brain that danger is imminent. The body then reacts accordingly. This signaling is automatic.

Furthermore, reacting to a trigger isn't always illogical. Some triggers actually do pose some type of threat. The situation may not be as dangerous as during the original trauma. But it could still lead to a major loss. Even someone without PTSD would be stressed by it. Yet for survivors, both physically and emotionally, it feels like being thrust back into the life-or-death world of their original trauma.

Darnell, for example, began having nightmares after an Arab family moved next door. Darnell liked them very much, especially since they'd been pro-American during the Iraq war. Yet the smell of their food put him into combat mode. Darnell felt his reaction to the family was "crazy" because he knew they were kindly. Yet eventually he relocated because his reactions to them were so strong he feared that someday he might lose control and hurt one of them.

On the other hand, Darnell's fury and terror upon hearing about his condo's new no-pet policy was not so "crazy." Darnell's dog had saved his life once, and in Iraq dogs had been used to find toxic substances and other dangers. Also, after his first wife divorced him and before meeting his second wife, his dog was practically the only form of love in his life.

After losing so many friends in Iraq, Darnell didn't think he could bear losing his dog without "going under." Yet he couldn't afford to move again. Hence the no-pet policy posed a real threat to Darnell's mental health.

Hyperarousal and PTSD

Fight-flight responses, often referred to as hyperarousal, can expand lung capacity, thereby increasing oxygen flow to the brain. Thus hyperarousal can sharpen mental abilities. But it can also lead to tunnel vision (intense focus on select aspects of the situation). Hence a crime victim might remember details about an assailant's gun, but not his face.

If the trauma is too long or severe, whatever positive effects adrenaline and noradrenaline might have on mental abilities can quickly disappear. Even under nontraumatic conditions, stress can cause memory and concentration problems, such as those that occur during test anxiety and stage fright. But when stresses pile up, or under conditions of trauma, our thoughts can become so scattered and our emotions so intense that it's almost impossible to focus or think logically.

Even everyday stresses can make us forget a good friend's birthday. If the stress continues, we might forget our mother's birthday. Yet under conditions of trauma or PTSD hyperarousal, we could even forget our own birthday! Hyperarousal can also lead to stress-related physical symptoms that further cloud our mental abilities—symptoms such as sweating, dizziness, nausea, headaches, backaches, hyperventilation, shortness of breath, choking sensations, hives, and muscle spasms.

Fight-flight responses lead to the insomnia, hypervigilance, and other symptoms listed under criterion E of PTSD (the "hyperarousal criterion"). Because the anxiety experienced during fight-flight responses in the present is similar to the anxiety experienced during the trauma, it can also bring forth memories of the trauma. This leads to the intrusive thoughts and nightmares of criterion B (the "reliving criterion") and the negative thinking and moods of criterion D.

Overreactivity

Fight-flight responses sharpen the senses, thereby increasing a person's sensitivity to sounds, smells, temperature, and touch. This sharpening of the senses provides people in danger with potentially lifesaving information. But it also makes it harder for them to handle noise, crowds, and situations full of many sights, smells, and activities in their current life.

For most people, the increased sensory arousal involved in parades, festivals, and similar events can be pleasurable and exciting. But for survivors, it can create a sensory overload, leading to unwanted F-F-F reactions.

Hyperarousal also opens the floodgates to all the pain, anger, confusion, terror, and other emotions associated with the original trauma. These feelings are difficult to manage even in mild form. But when they originate in the life-or-death circumstances of trauma, they're among the most intense feelings known to human beings.

Survivors are often terrified by the strength of their emotions. Experiencing them can feel as if, once again, they're being overpowered by a force greater than themselves, not of their choosing. It doesn't help that our culture tends to view emotional reactivity as a sign of immaturity or lack of self-control. Hence your partner may be angry at, or ashamed of, himself for having such strong feelings or for having a particular emotion that is thought to be undesirable or "bad." He may also fear that the sheer intensity of his emotions will scare people away.

His condemning attitudes toward his feelings and his fears of rejection increase the emotional pressure he is experiencing. He may then overreact to situations, perhaps creating a crisis when there wasn't one before. A soldier's quick-action response to the slightest hint of danger may be absolutely essential on the battlefield. But reacting explosively to small errors made by his wife will not serve him well.

NOW-OR-NEVER THINKING

Contributing to this overreactivity is the "now-or-never" thinking born from trauma. During many traumas there is little time to gather information and consider alternatives before deciding what to do or who can be trusted. Since even a few seconds could make the difference between life and death, decisions often need to be made on the spot. Hence some survivors feel they need to react immediately even when the situation isn't urgent.

Numbing Reactions and PTSD

Numbing can be a lifesaver during trauma. But when numbing is severe (either during the trauma or triggered afterward), it can create some of the same problems with concentration, memory, and clear thinking as those caused by hyperarousal. For example, sometimes

Darnell's mind shuts down so much he can't remember what he just read or heard. Following written directions and having conversations then becomes difficult. Intimacy becomes even more difficult because in close relationships even the slightest degree of emotional numbing can cause major problems.

Numbing can lead to dozing off when not tired, or to feeling like an observer to the point that one feels like a robot. Some survivors "lose time." Darnell, for example, missed his therapy appointment—not because he didn't want go, but because he couldn't find his keys. His inability to find the keys reminded him of a time when he couldn't find a grenade in time to save a buddy. This reminder plunged him into a state of nonbeing that lasted for hours. By the time Darnell returned to reality, he'd missed not only his therapy appointment, but also his daughter's piano recital. He then felt like even more of a failure.

Numbing can lessen—and sometimes entirely block out—not only painful feelings, memories, and physical sensations, but pleasurable and fulfilling ones as well. The loss of these positive feelings and memories can lead to despair, lack of motivation, alienation from others, and other symptoms listed under criterion D for PTSD.

When hyperarousal causes survivors to react to situations with an emotional intensity and style appropriate to their original trauma, they may be seen as "touchy" or "overly dramatic," "freaking out" over nothing. Yet when their numbing reactions cause them to underreact (or not react at all), they may be seen as "uncaring," "self-absorbed," or "selfish," leaving others feeing angry and abandoned.

Avoidance

Being triggered can be so physically uncomfortable, mentally confusing, and emotionally intense that survivors often avoid thoughts, conversations, and circumstances that might trigger them. Since the state of being stressed is a reminder of the trauma, survivors often avoid *any* situation that might cause stress, such as dealing with a relationship or financial issue.

Your partner may be avoiding certain situations and topics to protect himself from being triggered. But his avoidance also limits his options, hurts his self-esteem, and can negatively affect you. Perhaps, in turn, you feel burdened by the need to protect him from being triggered, or you resent the restrictions his avoidance puts on your lives.

People who don't understand PTSD may view him as "antisocial" or "abnormal." Unfortunately, if he has fears about being unworthy of love or about never being able to fit into society again, such views can drive him further into isolation.

The Unique Feature of PTSD: The PTSD Cycle

Some PTSD symptoms—such as sleep disturbances, irritability, and anxiety—are also signs of depression or other psychiatric illnesses. The unique feature of PTSD, however, is the PTSD cycle. In this cycle, the reliving of a trauma (the hyperalert stage) is followed by attempts to avoid or numb the memories, emotions, and physical sensations associated with the trauma (the numbing/avoidance stage).

At first glance, it doesn't seem logical that these two sets of opposite symptoms (one set associated with fight-flight reactions and the other, with freeze reactions) are part of the same diagnosis. Yet they are interrelated in that the hyperalert stage inevitably leads to the "shutdown" stage. Simply put, the human body can't tolerate prolonged periods of hyperalertness. Nor can the human psyche endure the mighty flood of emotions associated with reliving experiences over and over. Eventually exhaustion sets in, resulting in a physical and emotional "crash," or shutdown.

Darnell explains, "I hate feeling dead inside. But it's better than feeling like a human volcano." He doesn't consciously decide to make himself numb after having nightmares. It happens automatically.

Yet numbing, like hyperarousal, can be painful. Numbing refers to the shutting off or lessening of emotion. But survivors can be quite aware that they aren't having the emotions they used to have, or that others might be having. This awareness can make them feel inadequate and less than human. Hence their shutdown phases are usually followed by efforts to arouse themselves enough to feel more alive or to meet their responsibilities. But when another trigger comes along, the cycle begins again, leading to the "ups" and "downs" typical of PTSD.

The numbing stage generally lasts longer than the hyperarousal stage because it's usually easier to keep functioning when numb than it is to keep functioning when hyperaroused. During hyperarousal, survivors feel as if electricity is flowing through their veins, and they're terrified of losing emotional control. Functioning is almost impossible. But during numbing, at least some functioning is possible—provided the numbing isn't too severe.

For example, when Darnell is in the numbing stage, he works at a slower pace. But he can finish his work by staying late. During the hyperalert stage, however, his mind is bombarded with so many intrusive thoughts that he doesn't go to work. "Why bother? I can't focus," he explains. "And what if I overreact and go off on someone, or have a panic attack while driving and cause an accident?"

Addiction

Survivors can manage their PTSD by using coping techniques learned from therapy, self-help groups, and self-help books; by following various spiritual disciplines or family and cultural traditions; or by becoming involved in positive activities. But some survivors haven't had the chance to learn healthy ways of dealing with their PTSD and seek relief in alcohol, drugs, or another addiction.

Alcohol, certain drugs, and excess food can actually help reduce the insomnia, nightmares, anxiety, and irritability of the hyperalert stage of the PTSD cycle. They can also serve as "pick-me-ups" during the shutdown stage. But in the long run, addictions have a rebound effect and symptoms worsen. In the meantime, addictions create an additional set of medical, financial, and relationship problems that only worsen a survivor's existing problems.

Misdiagnosis

High rates of alcohol and drug abuse have been found among combat veterans and survivors of natural catastrophes, sexual assault, and other forms of interpersonal violence. Many survivors also suffer from clinical depression (Regel and Joseph 2010). When addiction or depression masks PTSD, the PTSD can go undetected. Often PTSD symptoms don't emerge until the addiction or depression has been treated. Yet if PTSD therapy isn't readily available, the recovering addict can easily resume her addiction to medicate her PTSD. Then, once again, her PTSD may be missed.

Other times PTSD goes unnoticed because survivors hesitate to talk about their trauma, or downplay their symptoms. They fear being disbelieved or being seen as "crazy." In the past, and to a lesser extent today, the auditory and visual flashbacks of PTSD have sometimes been mistaken for schizophrenia; and the mood swings of the PTSD cycle have been seen as signs of bipolar disorder. Similarly, the irritability and trust issues of survivors have sometimes been viewed as symptoms of borderline personality disorder, antisocial personality disorder, or some other negative-sounding disorder.

On the other hand, some survivors are diagnosed with PTSD when they're actually suffering from an undiscovered closed head injury or some other undiagnosed medical problem with similar symptoms (Morrison 1997).

Potential Health Consequences of PTSD

The adrenal system was designed for emergencies lasting for two or three days, not for weeks, months, or years of reacting to triggers. Depending on their frequency and severity, repeated surges of fight-flight hormones can harm various organs of the body, especially the heart. So it's no surprise that during the Civil War what we now call PTSD was called "soldier's heart" because of the great number of soldiers with cardiac pain, rapid pulse, and other heart problems. In World War I the epidemic of shortness of breath and heart problems among shell-shocked French and English soldiers was called DAH, or "disordered action of the heart." Yet often, no organic heart disease could be found (Shepard 2003).

The heart, respiratory, and digestive disorders suffered by soldiers, both then and now, have been linked to their adrenaline surges and to the physical strains of combat duty, such as sleep deprivation and exposure to extreme temperatures. Consequently, today, as in the past, combat soldiers tend not to live as long as military staff who never see combat (Shepard 2003).

Survivors of other traumas, especially domestic violence, rescue operations, and natural catastrophes, may have also endured long periods of physical hardship. Yet even people whose trauma didn't involve extreme physical stress are at risk for developing heart problems and stress-related illnesses such as peptic ulcers, skin problems, asthma, bronchitis, and repeated urinary and bladder infections. Obesity has been linked to childhood trauma (Dedert et al. 2010). Increased incidents of fibromyalgia, irritable bowel syndrome, and reproductive health problems have also been found among women with PTSD (Seng, et al. 2006).

The role of repeated surges of fight-flight hormones in causing medical problems has yet to be determined. It has been shown, however, that exposure to multiple traumas, contact with toxic substances, and trauma-related physical injuries weaken the immune system. And weakening of the immune system reduces resistance to other illnesses (Nazarian, Kimerling, and Frayne 2012).

Numerous studies show that people who have PTSD have more health problems than those who don't (Matsakis 2007). It isn't clear, however, how much these unhappy research findings reflect financial limitations, problems finding good health care, the effects of long-term substance abuse, or the unwillingness of some survivors to seek medical care due to low self-esteem or survivor guilt. Hopefully survivors who learn to manage their trigger reactions and have access to quality health care services can prevent other health problems. For the severely injured, however, certain conditions may be permanent.

Self-Esteem

The inner chaos created by the PTSD cycle is enough to shatter anyone's self-esteem. The firefighter who can't read bedtime stories to his child without remembering the charred bodies of other children often feels like an inadequate father. He wonders if his daughter senses what he's feeling, and why his love for her isn't stronger than his memories. His guilt about not being able to pay full attention to her only increases his guilt about not having saved certain other children.

The attorney whose husband committed suicide, who can't be as productive as she used to be, also suffers a blow to her self-esteem. Her need to hide her problems lest she lose even more self-respect puts a barrier between her and others. Like many survivors, she feels like "damaged goods" and a social outcast because she's been forever changed by her journey to another country—one that most of the people she knows have never been to and would never want to visit.

Blame-the-Victim Attitudes

Survivors who are surrounded by supportive others are fortunate. In contrast, many survivors are told that they brought the trauma on themselves, or are looked down upon or blamed for having PTSD.

But even survivors who are lovingly embraced by others can't escape the blame-the-victim attitudes still prevalent in our society. In part, these attitudes stem from the popular belief that the world is basically safe, orderly, and fair. Hence if one is careful, moral, and competent enough, one can prevent bad things from happening to oneself or others. This "just world" philosophy leads to the idea that "what goes around comes around," or that negative events are punishments for bad behavior.

It's difficult even for the most cared-about survivor to avoid being infected by society's blaming attitudes, especially if there is something that she feels she could have done to prevent the trauma. Trauma can also give rise to strong feelings of revenge, anger, self-hate, or self-doubt. These feelings can undercut a survivor's former view of herself as emotionally controlled, loving, and socially well adjusted. Her resulting low self-worth and separateness from others are only worsened by the stigma of a mental illness label like PTSD.

Even family members and friends who don't blame her for somehow causing the trauma may fault her for not recovering faster. In their view, her inability to quickly recover is due to her self-pity, laziness, desire for attention, or refusal to "lighten up."

Perhaps they feel frustrated and helpless as they watch someone they care about suffer. Or perhaps they don't appreciate how hard it is to recover from PTSD because they don't realize that trauma can affect almost every aspect of a person's life.

Trauma can also challenge previously held religious and spiritual beliefs about the meaning of life, often leading to considerable soul-searching and philosophical questioning. Yet such serious topics are not always popular in a society in which people tend to want—and expect—life to be enjoyable most of the time.

Blaming attitudes are more commonly held toward victims of family violence, sexual assault, and other individual traumas than toward victims of natural catastrophes or national tragedies. Yet even natural-catastrophe survivors sometimes feel responsible for some aspect of their trauma. Some are even told that if only they had done this and not that, the negative outcome could have been averted.

Attitudes Toward Suffering

In our society people who suffer for more than a few months are often viewed, and come to view themselves, as somehow defective and in need of therapy (Jay 2001). In other cultures, however, there is widespread acceptance of the fact that life includes both joy and sorrow. For example, in Buddhist and Hindu thinking and in many southern European, South American, and Middle Eastern cultures, suffering is considered unavoidable and is less likely to be seen as a sign of mental illness.

In these cultures there is no such thing as suffering "too much." Perhaps this is the case because these cultures have experienced so many invasions and other disasters that traumatic reactions are considered almost normal.

Indeed the first goal of trauma therapy is to "normalize" PTSD by assuring survivors that PTSD is a normal reaction to an abnormal amount of stress. In nations that have undergone centuries of trauma, PTSD is normalized not only in therapy, but in literature, music, and art. Various religious and social traditions not only openly recognize the agony involved in trauma, but honor it. Some also provide survivors with means of purification and reentering society (Jay 2001).

While people in these cultures suffer from the same symptoms, their cultures' acceptance of suffering makes them feel less alone with their pain. In our society, by contrast, a survivor's sense of isolation is increased by the idea that suffering is so shameful that it should be kept private (Jay 2001). So the survivor is expected to share her pain only with a therapist or with a few trusted friends.

Kat Duff (1993) notes that Western society values "heroic qualities," such as "activity, productivity, independence, strength, confidence, and optimism" (40). It doesn't respect qualities associated with PTSD, such as "quiet introspection, withdrawal, vulnerability, dependence, self-doubt, and depression" (41–42). These attitudes, Duff notes, tend to shame people in emotional pain. It's noteworthy that people who aren't made to feel ashamed or guilty because they hurt generally develop fewer long-term scars from traumatic events.

Possible Positive Outcomes Resulting from PTSD

On a more positive note, a growing number of studies show that sometimes trauma can lead to personal growth and stronger relationships (Joseph 2011). This doesn't mean that survivors can get back everything that they lost or be the people they were before their ordeals. Some areas of their lives may be permanently scarred. Yet they may be more determined than ever to achieve their life goals, take care of themselves, and be involved with loved ones and perhaps their communities as well.

Indeed, some survivors have achieved a degree of life satisfaction, emotional and spiritual growth, and caring for others that might have been impossible had they not been traumatized. Some report increased self-reliance and self-understanding, better ability to cope with crises and to tolerate uncertainty, and more appreciation for close relationships and the power of emotions (Stephen 2011).

When to Seek Help

PTSD symptoms are to be expected right after a trauma or upon recalling a previous trauma that had been forgotten or only partially remembered. If symptoms persist longer than thirty days, they meet the criteria for PTSD. It isn't necessary, however, to seek help immediately after the thirty-day cutoff if symptoms are sporadic, or if they seem to be tapering off.

Don't Overreact

There's wisdom in allowing a person time to process her trauma and regroup emotionally on her own for a while. Often, a person who has just experienced being powerless doesn't want to see a doctor or therapist because it feels as if, once again, she won't be in control. Any suggestion that she needs help because "something is wrong" with her can be infuriating, because something wrong was just done *to* her, or because she may already feel inadequate as a result of the trauma.

If your partner has just returned from a war zone or rescue mission, or from the trial of her attacker or her sister's murderer, or if she's going through a major life change, expect her symptoms to increase. Only time will tell which ones are serious and which are not.

Don't Underreact

While it is important not to panic, don't ignore obvious signs such as increased drinking or night after night of nightmares. If your partner's symptoms steadily worsen or her patterns of coping come to include verbal abuse, violence, addiction, or some other self-destructive behavior, then help is needed.

Don't rely solely your own opinions or on this or any other book. Before you come to any firm conclusions about her condition and what actions to take, consult with trusted others who care about her, *and* also with a mental health professional with expertise in PTSD.

Chronic PTSD

If her symptoms last more than three months, she's considered to have chronic PTSD. If she doesn't get help, her chronic PTSD could turn into longer-term PTSD. After three months, the longer she waits to seek help, the more her symptoms can develop a life of their own and come to dominate even the more functioning aspects of her life—and yours. (See chapter 7 for suggestions on encouraging your partner to seek help.)

Emergencies

If, at any time, your partner (or anyone in your household) becomes suicidal, homicidal, or out of control in any way, or displays any of the symptoms listed in the Cautions section in the introduction to this book, you'll need to take charge. Follow the recommendations and get help immediately. Chapter 6 provides guidelines for handling rage reactions and other crises until you're able to get outside help.

Understanding the many ways PTSD can affect your partner is an important first step toward supporting her and improving your relationship. You can learn more about PTSD through some of the resources listed at the end of this book. In chapter 2, you'll identify the ways PTSD has affected your relationship and ways you'd like the relationship to improve.

CHAPTER 2

PTSD and Your Relationship

In this chapter you'll begin looking at some of your hopes and dreams for your relationship. You'll start by writing the story of your relationship—how it began and the reasons you continue loving your partner. You'll then be asked to do some thinking and writing about how your partner's PTSD affects your relationship and the specific ways you'd like your relationship to improve.

Answering some of the questions in the upcoming exercises might require considerable time, effort, and soul-searching. It may also be quite difficult. But remember that your thoughtful responses will help point you in the direction of the improvements you hope to make in your life.

The Courage to Love

It takes courage to love, writes psychologist Rollo May (1994). Courage is needed, he explains, because loving someone means opening yourself up to that person. Intimate relationships require the most courage, May emphasizes. Why? Because in order to have genuine intimacy, you need to open yourself up to your partner on an ongoing basis.

You must also be willing to take two huge risks, May says. The first risk is that your partner might reject you. Hence the outcome of all your caring efforts is uncertain—and even temporary rejections can be very wounding. The second risk is that you might feel suffocated by his needs and wants. At times you may feel so overwhelmed by his expectations of you that you fear you're losing your personal identity for his sake.

Taking such risks, as May stresses, requires considerable inner strength. Even under the best of circumstances, trying to establish and maintain an emotionally and physically rewarding relationship is full of challenges. Loving someone with PTSD, moreover, requires a special kind of courage and dedication. PTSD complicates many of the normal challenges couples face. It also creates an additional set of problems. But remember—your love for your partner must be deep. Otherwise you wouldn't still be with him, trying to make things better by reading this book.

The Courage to Be Honest

Completing the exercises in this chapter and the rest of this book will require yet another kind of courage: the courage to be honest with yourself. As you complete these exercises, try to set aside what others may have told you about what you should or shouldn't want from a relationship. Focus instead on your unique desires, needs, and goals. Since you don't have to share your journal with anyone, you can be truthful as you wish.

Learning about yourself and your relationship is a process. Accordingly, a few hours (or days or weeks) after answering a particular question, you may become aware of some additional truths about yourself, your partner, or your relationship. You can then return to your journal entry for that particular question and revise or add to it.

Mixed Feelings

As you write about your relationship, don't be surprised if you discover you have mixed feelings toward your partner. Love would be so much simpler if it weren't mixed in with times of resentment, jealousy, contempt, and other problematic emotions! Yet mixed feelings are a normal part of all relationships. This truth is especially evident in intimate relationships, where two people live together and have so much invested in each another.

You probably already know that having mixed feelings is perfectly normal. Yet writing about them can still be upsetting—and confusing. It's not always easy to tell which feelings are important and which ones can be safely overlooked. But don't add to your distress by deciding that having negative emotions toward your partner means that you don't really love him.

Doubt is a normal part of love. If the love weren't there, you probably wouldn't have bought this book and taken the time to read this far. Remember also that the reason you're willing to do the hard work of identifying your feelings toward your partner, including any unpleasant feelings you wish you didn't have, is in hopes of strengthening your relationship, not harming it.

Darnell's new wife, Nina, sometimes wonders if having mixed feelings toward Darnell means she's just not capable of having a long-term relationship. However having mixed feelings doesn't mean she's flawed or can't have a committed relationship. It doesn't automatically mean that her relationship is a failure or is doomed to fail, either.

Do you find yourself jumping to these or other unhappy conclusions? If so, maybe you're basing your conclusions on only a few aspects of your current situation and not taking into account the total picture.

You also may be forgetting about the possibility of positive change. Few situations are so hopeless that there isn't some action that can be taken to improve matters. Whatever miserable or disastrous ending you're imagining is only one of many possible outcomes.

EXERCISE 2.1: The Story of My Current Relationship

In order to better understand your hopes for your relationship, it helps to look at how it began and what has kept it going. On a separate page in your journal, entitled "The Story of My Current Relationship," answer the following questions:

1. How did you meet your partner?

2. What attracted you to him?

3. What made you decide to commit to him?

4. Did his trauma occur before or after you became involved with him?

5. When did his PTSD symptoms become evident?

    Perhaps his trauma occurred after you met him. Or perhaps he was traumatized before you met him, but displayed few PTSD symptoms. Often they begin to emerge as the relationship becomes increasingly intimate, or after marriage or the birth of a child.

    Some survivors may be emotionally exhausted from their trauma. This exhaustion can limit the amount of psychic energy they have available for relationships. As the relationship grows, so do its emotional—and often financial and other—demands. The resulting stress can bring previously hidden or underlying PTSD to the surface.

6. What do you appreciate about your partner now?

My Partner's PTSD Symptoms

The most common symptoms of PTSD include insomnia, nightmares, flashbacks, intrusive thoughts, anxiety, insecurity, guilt, depression, hopelessness, emotional numbing, irritability, anger, rage reactions, isolation, low self-worth, difficulties concentrating, substance abuse, social withdrawal, negativity, and periods of restlessness and hyperactivity followed by periods of withdrawal and apathy.

Yet PTSD symptoms vary from one individual to the next. Some survivors have a "short fuse" and are in a constant state of crisis. Others are generally unresponsive, or vary in their responsivity. Some are extremely dependent on their partners for emotional support and help in dealing with the outside world. Still others insist that they don't need any help at all.

Some partners assume additional responsibilities because of their survivor's problems. But others find that their survivor insists on taking charge of everything, and can do so with the utmost efficiency. Some partners fear that their survivor's anger will explode into violence; others, that the survivor's depression or substance abuse will end in suicide.

EXERCISE 2.2: Tracking My Partner's PTSD Symptoms

Your partner's symptoms are unique to her personality, trauma, and other life experiences. Based on what you've learned about PTSD, you can begin to form a picture of the unique ways PTSD expresses itself in your partner.

1. On a separate page in your journal, entitled "My Partner's PTSD Symptoms," list your partner's PTSD symptoms. Don't limit yourself to the symptoms described above. List as many as you wish. Refer back to chapter 1 if you need to.

2. Describe how each symptom you listed in number 1 affects your relationship. For example, if your partner has memory problems, do you have to remind her of appointments, or be the one who picks up the children? If she can't sleep at night, does this mean that you sleep in separate rooms, or that she can't keep a job because she's always late? Are you up half the night calming her down or changing sweaty sheets? If she avoids social gatherings, do you argue frequently about her unwillingness to attend family functions?

3. Review your list of your partner's symptoms, and rate each symptom on a scale of 1 to 5, with 1 meaning that the symptom is extremely disruptive and troublesome to you, and 5 meaning that the symptom isn't that upsetting to you.

4. Of all of her symptoms, which three distress you or disrupt your relationship the most?

The Emotional Impact of Your Partner's Symptoms

Perhaps you try to separate your partner's PTSD from his personality or from him as a person. But this isn't always easy, or possible. For example, when Darnell is irritable with Nina, she often tries to tell herself, "That's not Darnell. That's his PTSD." Although Nina tries to be understanding, Darnell's irritability pushes her away from him more than she likes to admit.

Yet Darnell's PTSD affects more than Nina's feelings toward Darnell. It affects her feelings toward herself. Sometimes his PTSD makes her feel guilty or inadequate. "If I were a better wife or could handle Darnell's symptoms better, he wouldn't be so restless and discontent," she tells herself. But at other times, the fact that she remains committed to Darnell despite his PTSD makes her feel proud of herself.

EXERCISE 2.3: How PTSD Affects My Feelings Toward My Partner, My Relationship, and Myself

On a separate page in your journal, entitled "How PTSD Affects My Feelings Toward My Partner, My Relationship, and Myself," answer the following questions:

1. How does each of the three main symptoms you identified in number 4 of exercise 2.2 affect your feelings toward your partner?

   Remember that having mixed feelings is normal. The same symptom can fill you with fear, disgust, or anger on one day, and with love and compassion the next. Or it can leave you feeling abandoned, betrayed, pissed off, bewildered, relieved, ashamed, or some mix of these or other emotions all at the same time.

2. How do your partner's top three symptoms affect your feelings about your relationship? For example, does her hypervigilance make you feel pessimistic, optimistic, skeptical, confused, or some other way about the future of your relationship?

3. How do her three main symptoms affect your feelings toward yourself? Maybe a particular symptom doesn't affect your self-image at all. Or maybe it makes you feel needed, unimportant, insecure, incompetent, or some other way.

4. How do you think these three symptoms affect your partner's feelings toward you, your relationship, or herself? Do you think a particular symptom makes her feel grateful for you, unworthy of you, abandoned by you, annoyed with you, or some mix of these and other emotions? Do any of her symptoms make her feel better about herself or your relationship?

The Importance of Positive Goals

As relationship experts John Gottman (1999) and Bernard Guerney (1987) point out, it's important for couples to work toward positive goals, rather than simply try to eliminate all their conflict areas. There will always be disagreements, these experts stress. But what distinguishes happy couples from unhappy ones is the number of positives in the relationship—for it is the positive times and feelings that sustain couples through their more difficult moments.

Toward the end of this chapter you'll be asked to identify some positive goals for your relationship. However, doing so may not be as easy as it sounds. So many hurts and resentments may have built up over the years that all you may want to do is stop the hurtful situations from repeating themselves.

EXERCISE 2.4: Recognizing My Resentments and Disappointments

In order to have a clearer picture of how you'd like your relationship to be, you may first need to identify your resentments. On a separate page in your journal, entitled "My Resentments and Disappointments," list the things you resent about your partner and the things that have disappointed you in your relationship. Or write your partner a letter telling him exactly how you feel about him and all the ways he has disappointed you.

Express yourself freely. Don't hold back. But don't share your list or letter with your partner either. After finishing this exercise, you can throw it away if you want.

It could take you ten minutes or ten days to write your letter or list, depending on how many grievances you have. Don't be surprised if you have more anger and hurt than you thought. Over the years you may have buried much of it, and as you begin writing about one of your grievances, the memory of another may suddenly emerge.

This process can be quite emotional. It is, therefore, a good idea to limit your work on your letter or list to no more than twenty minutes a day.

Uncovering Your Deepest Hopes and Wishes for Your Relationship

Underlying each experience of frustration and anger you wrote about in exercise 2.4 is an unfulfilled longing or need. For example, if you're angry because your partner doesn't spend enough time with you, it probably means that you enjoy being with him and you miss him. In other words, the negative feelings and relationship problems you identify can point you toward what you really want from your partner.

EXERCISE 2.5: Establishing Positive Goals for My Relationship

After completing exercise 2.4, set it aside for a day or two. Then review your letter or list of grievances. Pay special attention to any parts that made you feel like crying, or like never talking to your partner again. Circle those parts and spend some time thinking about the hopes and dreams that underlie your anger or sadness.

Then, on a separate page in your journal, entitled "My Goals for My Relationship," answer the following questions:

1. Was there ever a time when you didn't have so much pain and anger? Write a few sentences—or paragraphs, if you wish—about what those times were like. Describe your sadness and other feelings about the fact that those times are fewer now.

47

2. Think about the beginning of your relationship and what attracted to your partner, as you described in exercise 2.1. Are there aspects of the beginning of the relationship you wish still existed? Is it possible to recreate some of these aspects? If so, how could that happen? Write a few sentences about what it would take to revive them, even in part.

3. Based on what you've learned about your deepest needs and wishes for your relationship, write a few paragraphs about what your relationship would look like if it met those needs and wishes.

4. Given the hopes for your relationship you that described in this exercise, what are the three most important ways you'd like your relationship to improve?

5. Write a few sentences about each of the three major relationship goals you identified in number 4, above. (Include only goals related to PTSD.) Be as specific as possible.

Congratulations! You've just completed a great deal of emotional work! If you're feeling exhausted from the effort, take a break and do something pleasurable or rewarding.

The Importance of Communication

Regardless of the kind of goals you have for your relationship, good communication is essential. It's therefore highly recommended that you read and complete the exercises in chapter 3, "Basic Communication Skills," and chapter 4, "Talking About Difficult Subjects and Making Decisions Together."

CHAPTER 3

Basic Communication Skills

"Communication is a lot of work," sighs Paul, whose wife Kitty grew up in a violent home. "Kitty has a lot of triggers and I never know when something I say will set her off. Sometimes she's perfectly reasonable and we can find a solution to a problem very quickly. But other times, she'll throw up her hands and say, 'I can't deal with this now,' in a way that tells me she's stressed out by her past.

"'Let's talk later,' she says. But even if we set a time, that doesn't mean she'll feel like talking then. If I pressure her to talk, she'll just get mad or not talk to me for days. I know she loves me, but when she acts that way it sure doesn't feel like it.

"My first girlfriend was like Kitty. She didn't have PTSD, but if she was stressed, she'd blow me off when I wanted to talk. But it was different with her. When I'd insist on talking and she'd flare up or walk out of the room, I felt bad. But I never felt guilty. With Kitty, though, I feel like I've shoved her back into the hell of her childhood where she was terrified, sad, and lonely, and where it wasn't safe to be close to people. Once it took weeks for her to come back to the here-and-now and let me in again.

"I don't want to be responsible for that! So now when I'm about to say something to Kitty, sometimes I stop myself. But we have to talk sometime, don't we? Isn't communication what a relationship is all about?"

Like Paul, you may find communicating with your partner difficult and frustrating. You might also find yourself with the same dilemma: You want to talk to your partner because you want to feel closer to her, or because you make decisions about your finances or some other aspect of your life together. Yet sometimes trying to communicate with her only pushes her away, and you're left hanging.

Communication is especially difficult when every conversation holds the possibility of setting off the dreaded PTSD cycle (described in chapter 1). But communication is a problem for many couples, even those free of PTSD. Perhaps, like most couples, you and your mate were never taught the communication skills necessary for a love relationship. Having a relationship in which both partners feel cared about and supported requires what's called "positive communication."

Positive communication involves listening carefully to what your partner is saying and making sure you heard her correctly. It also involves trying to understand what she's feeling, showing your concern when she's hurting, and sharing her joy when something good happens to her. Both of you need to be able to talk to each other without fear of being ignored, unfairly criticized, or ridiculed, and without putting your partner down (Fisher, Giblin, and Hoopes 1982).

In this chapter you'll learn about positive communication skills and how to use them with someone with PTSD. You'll also learn about some unhealthy ways of communicating, and will be asked to do some writing about the positive and negative ways you and your partner interact. You'll then apply the skills you've learned to your communication problems. In chapter 4, "Talking About Difficult Subjects and Making Decisions Together," you'll learn how to use these skills when discussing your relationship conflicts and other sensitive issues.

In all relationships, but especially intimate ones, communication is key. But communication is a two-way street. You can learn all the skills in this chapter, but that doesn't mean your partner will communicate with you as you'd like.

The hope is that by improving the way you relate to her, she'll feel safer and more open to talking with you. The more the two of you talk, the closer you'll become. Another hope is that she'll want to learn some of these skills along with you. But even if she doesn't, she can't help but learn some of them simply by interacting with you.

Learning Communication Skills

Learning communication skills isn't easy. At first it may take a lot of self-control to not interrupt your partner when you disagree with him. It'll take even more effort to make sure you heard him correctly.

It's worth the effort, because being truly heard and understood can have a softening effect. Once you see this softening effect in your partner, you'll realize that your efforts made a positive difference. Your attempts to listen to him more carefully and with more compassion will also show him how much you care about him. Perhaps, at times, he seems immune to love. But if he didn't want love in his life, he wouldn't be in a relationship with you; he'd be one of the many survivors who, for any number of reasons, choose to live alone.

Being Authentic

Perhaps you think that using communication skills means you can't say how you really feel. But using communication skills doesn't mean stifling yourself. It means expressing your thoughts and feelings, even your negative ones, in ways that show respect for your partner and help you feel good about yourself too. For example, there's a big difference between screaming "You ungrateful loser! No wonder your first husband left you!" (or "No wonder you have nightmares!") and firmly stating that "I'm so angry I feel like cursing you!"

None of the skills in this chapter will work unless you sincerely want to understand your partner and are honest about your own emotions. It's always best to be real and not put on an act, especially when communicating with survivors.

Survivors, especially survivors of child abuse and family violence, can be very good at picking up on what someone's thinking or feeling but not saying. Many have been betrayed so many times during or after their trauma that they're on the lookout for signs of insincerity and falseness in others. If your partner, like Kitty, is a survivor of childhood trauma or of adult domestic violence, then she'll be especially on guard for the slightest hint that you don't mean what you say.

Sometimes, however, you may choose not to express a thought or emotion. Maybe the timing isn't good or maybe you have another reason. Authentic expression means that you can choose not to share something, and if your partner asks, you have the right to tell her you choose not to share that information with her.

The section titled "Guidelines for Effective Self-Expression," later in this chapter, can help you express your thoughts and feelings, or your decision not to share them, constructively rather than destructively.

The "No Secrets" Rule

As a child, Kitty tried to predict her father's attacks, just like military officers try to predict enemy plans and maneuvers. Sometimes

Kitty knew what was coming and could hide. But sometimes her father's attacks came out of nowhere.

All traumas involve one or more unexpected horrible events. Consequently many survivors don't like surprises. Some survivors seem to like the thrill of the unknown and seek adventure, but they are in the minority. Most want to feel safe at all costs, and for them, surprises aren't safe.

If following the suggestions in this book changes the usual ways you relate to your partner, she might become anxious. She might even think you're being phony, "acting like a shrink," or trying to manipulate her. It's important, therefore, to tell her about the ideas in this book before trying them out with her. If she's curious, show her this book and invite her comments.

"No secrets" is an important rule to remember in your relationship. Lies, deception, and cover-ups are a part of many traumas. Your partner may have a strong negative reaction to what seems like a small change in routine, just because she didn't know about it first.

Even a positive change could startle or upset her. For example, when Paul tried to improve his marriage by complimenting Kitty more often, Kitty shrank away from him. For her, extra compliments had a terrible meaning. In the past, Kitty's father had used flattery to manipulate her, lavishing her with compliments before locking her up in rooms and assaulting her.

Had Paul told Kitty why he was planning to be more attentive, she might not have assumed the worst when he upped the amount of appreciation he showed her. She would also have had the chance to tell Paul that his idea, although lovely, might not work for her. Then he would have been spared the hurt of being rejected for doing something so caring.

A "no secrets" policy doesn't mean you have to report to your partner. She doesn't own you. But in matters concerning your relationship, giving her a heads-up can avoid a future blowup. It also gives her the opportunity to give you feedback on your idea. That way you know whether to try it, reject it, or change it in a way that will help your relationship rather than hurt it.

Practicing Communication Skills

Learning communication skills requires practicing them until they feel natural. Start out using them with friends or while talking with your partner about everyday matters. Wait until you're familiar and comfortable with these skills before using them to discuss major problems.

TAILORING COMMUNICATION SKILLS

The techniques in this chapter are recommended by many couples therapists and self-help books on communication. Some have been changed, however, in order to take into account your partner's PTSD. You'll also need to tailor the suggestions to your and your partner's individual personalities and histories. Experiment until you find those that work best for the two of you.

Even a highly recommended method could backfire if it's associated with a negative event for one of you. For example, when someone's feeling low, reminding him about his concrete achievements is often suggested as a way of being supportive. Yet when Nina tried to encourage Darnell by reminding him of his Medal of Honor, he sulked for days.

Although Darnell earned this medal for saving lives, during the same incident he also made errors that cost lives. But Nina didn't know this. She then tried to cheer him up by reminding him of how he'd been repeatedly selected for special training. "Don't you dare call me smart!" he shouted. "If I'm so smart, how come I have PTSD?"

From then on, before trying out an idea from a talk show or self-help book, Nina ran it past Darnell first to make sure it wasn't booby-trapped with traumatic memories.

EXERCISE 3.1: Learning from the Past

Like Nina and Paul, you may be unaware of all the topics or ways of communicating that might prove unhelpful in your relationship. But you're probably aware of some of them. You've also probably had some positive communication experiences with your partner as well. In the following exercise, you'll be writing about instances of both successful and unsuccessful communication with your partner. You'll then be asked to think about what helped make these interactions successful or unsuccessful.

On a separate page in your journal, entitled "Learning from the Past: Successful and Unsuccessful Communications," follow these instructions:

1. Reflecting back on your relationship, were there any times when you and your partner resolved a major difference, cooperated during a crisis, or grew closer by talking over your differences? Write a few sentences about two or three of these times. Describe the time, the place, the topic discussed, and the ways that you and your partner talked to each other.

2. For each instance of successful communication described in number 1, what do you think made things go smoothly? Did outside factors (circumstances unrelated to your or your partner's personality—such as the location, the time of the day or year, the presence or absence of others) make a difference? When the situation became tense, what did you or your partner do or say (or not do or say) that stopped your meeting from becoming a screaming match or a stalemate? Did either of you use any skills learned from a self-help book or therapist that helped? If so, which ones?

3. Now write about two or three times when your talks failed or created even more problems. Note the time, place, topic, and any especially tense or painful moments.

4. Think about each unsuccessful conversation you described in number 3. Was there anything about the time or place that created problems? In each instance, what did you or your partner say or do (or not say or do) that contributed to your communication breakdown? Describe any techniques that either of you used that didn't seem to help.

   Later on in this chapter, you'll have the chance to return to these instances of communication breakdown and rework them using positive communication skills.

   You'll now use what you've learned from the past to make several lists.

5. Based on your replies to number 2 and number 4, on a separate page in your journal, entitled "Outside Factors Affecting Communication," make a list of all the outside factors that seem to affect your communication with your partner. Put a plus sign next to those that seem to help and a minus sign next to those that don't. (You'll refer to this list when you learn about setting up a time and place to discuss serious issues with your partner, in chapter 4.)

6. Review your replies to number 2 and number 4 again. Then, on a separate page in your journal, entitled "Ways I Communicate That Work Well for My Partner," list words, gestures, and any ways of talking to your partner that have had good results.

7. On a separate page in your journal, entitled "Ways I Communicate That Don't Work Well for My Partner," list the words, gestures, and ways you've talked with your partner that haven't had good results.

8. On a separate page in your journal, entitled "Ways My Partner Communicates That Work Well for Me," list the ways he talks to you that you like and respond well to.

9. On a separate page in your journal, entitled "Ways My Partner Communicates That Don't Work Well for Me," list the ways he talks to you that you don't like or that aren't helpful.

Congratulations! You've taken some major steps toward developing your own personal communication "dos and don'ts" based on your experiences. As you work through this book, you'll be referring to these lists and adding to them.

Communicating About Communicating

At some point, you might want to share your lists with your partner. But first you need to learn the skills described in the rest of this chapter and in the following chapter. Otherwise you may not be able to present and discuss the information on your lists effectively.

After learning these skills, if you decide to share your lists with your partner, don't overload him by presenting all of them in the same sitting. Share a few entries at a time. Begin with those you feel would be the least threatening to him, and with which he'd be most likely to agree. However, if you feel that, even with the help of your new skills, sharing parts of your list might start a big argument, then don't.

Rewarding Positive Communication

In your journal entry titled "Ways My Partner Communicates That Work Well for Me," you listed approaches that you like. When you notice him speaking to you in one of these ways, consider rewarding him. Tell him how much you appreciate it. If you want, mention times in the past when he talked to you the same way and what a positive difference it made.

For example, you could say, "I really appreciate your giving up your favorite show to hear me out. It reminds me of that time when you were crazy busy, but let me talk as long as I needed. That meant a lot to me and it still does." Or, "Thanks for not making a big deal about that mean comment I made tonight. It was wrong of me, and it was big of you to cut me some slack. Remember those wisecracks I made when we were doing our taxes? If you hadn't let them slide, we would never have finished on time."

Notice how these comments differ from saying, "I can't believe you turned off the TV to talk to me. I thought I'd have to be half dead first!" Or, "You usually jump all over me when I make wisecracks, but tonight you were half human. Is this a once-in-a-lifetime event, or can I expect another miracle before I die?"

When Nina first began rewarding Darnell for talking to her in positive ways, she couldn't help also mentioning some of the negative ways he talked to her. But she soon realized that criticizing Darnell right after rewarding him lessened the power of her words of appreciation. As difficult as it may be, don't mention your partner's disagreeable communication habits when you're trying to reward him for his positive ones. How would you feel if he thanked you for something and then promptly reeled off a list of ways you've disappointed him?

Expressing Personal Preferences

If you want your partner to stop communicating with you in ways that upset you, telling him that you don't like how he is talking to you is not enough. Instead of scolding him, show him how you'd like him to talk to you.

Use your journal entry "Ways My Partner Communicates That Don't Work Well for Me" to begin teaching your partner how you'd like to be approached. When he speaks to you in disagreeable ways, say, "I'd really like it if you'd say it like this," and then give him an example.

Your journal entry "Ways I Communicate That Don't Work Well for My Partner" describes approaches that you know are not effective. Yet you might not know how to rephrase a request or bring up a particular subject in a way that would work better for him. If so, ask for a suggestion: "If I want to talk to you about this, what's the best (or an okay) way to do it?"

If the matter isn't urgent, it's important to add, "You can take some time to think about it." During his trauma he had few, if any, choices. So whenever it's possible and agreeable to you, give him some reasonable choices as to how or when to discuss a particular subject.

Pitfalls to Avoid

Name-calling and other kinds of ridicule let off steam, but they don't tell your partner what's really bothering you. They're more likely to make matters worse by leaving her feeling so lonely, angry, disgusted, or misunderstood that she'll be in no mood to listen to anything else you have to say. Then she'll either withdraw or retaliate in kind.

Avoid the following communication pitfalls at all costs:

- Name-calling: "You're a sicko." (Or "whiner," or "crybaby," or "fatso," or "drama queen," or "leech.")

- Shaming: "Where's your head?" "That's ridiculous," "My father didn't get PTSD," or "Only babies feel that way."

- Mocking your partner's trauma or blaming all of your relationship problems on PTSD: "You and your darn trauma!" or "Everything with you is a trigger! No wonder our relationship is going down the tubes."

- Nonverbal insults—offensive noises or gestures: playing an imaginary violin to show disgust when she's telling you about her trauma, touching your finger to your forehead to suggest that she's crazy, or raising your eyebrows in disbelief.

- Invalidating, denying, or minimizing her experience.

Invalidating your partner means letting her know that you think what she's saying or feeling isn't true or justifiable. For example, if you insist that she feels a way she says she doesn't feel or that she likes something she says she doesn't like, you're invalidating her: "You're angry but you just won't admit it," or "Come on, you know you really like it."

Another way to invalidate her is by telling her that the main reason she's thinking or feeling a particular way is that she's somehow inadequate or wrong about something—in other words: "You're only seeing things (or feeling) this way because you're overly sensitive." (Or "because you lack discipline," or "because you don't have the right attitude," or "because you aren't trying or praying hard enough.")

Advising her to "let go of the past" or "snap out of it," or offering her a slogan or unsolicited advice, can also feel invalidating. Suppose she were to claim that you don't have any real problems, or that you shouldn't be feeling sad or frustrated because you weren't traumatized like she was. Then she would be invalidating you.

Verbal Abuse

Insults, curses, and threats; making your partner feel guilty; holding her responsible for your or someone else's behavior; and making derogatory comments about her body, family, ethnic background, religion, friends, career, or any aspect of herself that she can't change or that she cherishes are all forms of verbal abuse. Obscene or threatening gestures are also abusive.

Verbal abuse is unacceptable. If your partner becomes verbally abusive, and if you feel it's safe for you to speak out, you can tell her that you'll talk to her only if she speaks to you respectfully. If her verbal abuse continues, or you start to become verbally abusive, call for a time-out. (For more about time-outs, see number 9 under "Getting Ready for Your Discussion" in chapter 4.)

EXERCISE 3.2: Communication Pitfalls

On a separate page in your journal, entitled "Communication Pitfalls," answer the following questions:

1. Which, if any, of the common communication pitfalls described above (name-calling, shaming, and so forth) have you fallen into during your relationship? (If you've managed to avoid them all, proceed to number 4 in this exercise.)

2. Describe a specific instance for each of the pitfalls you listed in number 1.

3. Write a few sentences about how the instances you described in number 2 might have influenced your feelings toward yourself, your partner, and your relationship. (For example, you may have hurt or angered your partner by calling him names. And speaking so disrespectfully to someone you love may have also saddened, angered, or upset you as well.)

4. Which, if any, of the common communication pitfalls described above has your partner fallen into during your relationship? (If your partner's behavior has been free of these pitfalls, skip the rest of this exercise.)

5. Describe a specific instance for each of the pitfalls you identified in number 4.

6. For each instance described in number 5, write a few sentences about its effects on your feelings toward yourself,
   your partner, and your relationship.

Later on in this chapter you'll be asked to return to these examples
and design more positive ways of expressing the same messages.

Active Listening

Communication involves two basic types of skills: listening skills and
expressive skills. Listening skills have to do with how you listen, and
expressive skills with how you express yourself. This section outlines
an important form of listening called "active" listening. It's called
active listening because you'll need to do more than listen as usual.

Active listening is usually described as having four basic steps:

1. Listening carefully to what your partner is saying and trying
   to understand his emotions

2. In a calm voice, reflecting what you've heard—in other words,
   giving your partner a summary of what you think he is saying
   and feeling

3. Showing concern for his difficulties and reacting positively to
   his happier moments

4. Repeating steps 1 to 3 until he feels you've understood both
   his message and his emotions

Steps 2, 3, and 4 aren't always necessary when you're talking about
ordinary matters. But they are essential when discussing important
ones. However, because your partner has PTSD, there are certain

times when aspects of these steps can make matters worse. If you learned about active listening from a self-help book or in couples therapy, you may notice that the suggestions below are somewhat different. That's because the usual guidelines for active listening have been changed to take into account your partner's PTSD.

Step 1: Listening and Observing

In order to listen carefully to your partner and let him know that what he's saying is important to you, consider the following suggestions.

PAY ATTENTION TO YOUR PARTNER

1. Turn off the TV. Ignore the computer, phone, or any other distractions. Face your partner, and lean toward him.

2. Even if he's telling you about something as routine as an appointment change, stop what you're doing and look at him.

3. Maintain eye contact during your entire conversation. Even if he isn't (or stops) looking at you, keep looking at him. Doing so acknowledges and honors his presence. It's also the only way you'll be able to note his body language, a valuable source of information about his emotional state.

4. If he isn't looking at you, consider asking him to do so. But if the topic is distressing, or he's told you (or you sense) that he's stressed or numb, let him be.

   If he's dealing with something difficult, he may be afraid that eye contact with you could heighten his emotions to the point that he enters the dreaded PTSD cycle. But if he's simply caught up in surfing the Internet, it's generally okay to ask him to look at you. If he won't, back off.

5. Don't fidget or look annoyed or uninterested. If you yawn, quickly explain that you're sleepy, not bored.

6. If you're expecting an important call, you're short on time, or you're not in the right frame of mind to deal with his message, say so early on. Then suggest a time to talk later.

GET THE FACTS STRAIGHT

1. Like a good newspaper reporter, you need to know the who, what, when, and where of his message. If he didn't say what date an appointment was changed to, find out the exact date later. As trivial as this example may sound, many arguments have sprung from failure to pin down the details.

2. Focus on what your partner is saying, not on whether he's right or wrong or really believes what he's saying. For the moment, assume that what he's saying is true (or true for him). You can correct him later, if necessary, but for now your job is to listen.

LET YOUR PARTNER TALK

1. In general, let your partner finish talking before asking questions, offering advice, or proceeding to step 2. Some Native American tribes use "talking sticks." Nobody else can speak until the person holding the stick sets it down to show that he is finished. Perhaps you could come up with your own type of talking stick, such as a hand signal that means "I'm done. Your turn." For example, you could tap your mouth a few times with your finger or put your hand over your mouth. If you're sitting, you could stand up for a few seconds and then sit down again, or vice versa.

2. If you feel you need to interrupt your partner for some necessary information, ask if it's okay: "I have a quick question. Should I ask, or wait?"

   Your question needs to be about his message and should concern an important part of his message, not an irrelevant detail. For example, suppose he says, "Mary insulted me." You probably need to know whether he's referring to Mary, the little girl next door, or Mary, his supervisor. But you don't need to know the color of Mary's dress.

   Consider coming up with a hand signal (such as raising a finger or tapping your ear) that means "I have a question about something you said. I only need a short answer, but I don't want to distract you. Is it okay to interrupt? If not, I can wait." For example, you could raise your hand, outline the shape of a question mark with your finger, or gently tap your ear. You could also use an object to indicate that you want to ask a short question. For example, you could turn over a piece of paper, an empty paper cup, or some other nonbreakable object. Your partner could simply nod "yes" or "no" as a reply.

   Using hand signals or small objects instead of words will be frequently recommended in this book. Deciding together on ways of communicating nonverbally helps unify you. Also, if either of you is stressed, it's easy to choose the wrong word or misinterpret the right word (or the way it is spoken).

NOTICE YOUR PARTNER'S FEELINGS

1. Pay special attention to any feelings he says he's experiencing.

2. Notice his body language. Pay attention to the tone, pitch, and volume of his voice; the pace of his speech; the way he's breathing or moving; his facial expressions; and his physical condition. What do you think these cues are telling you about his emotions?

Step 2: Reflecting

The second step usually involves reflecting back to your partner your understanding of his message and emotions. You don't need to reflect his every word or emotion—just the main parts of his message and his main emotions. Given your partner's PTSD, however, there are times when reflecting might not be helpful, or when the ways you reflect may need to be modified.

WHEN NOT TO REFLECT

1. You may know from experience that your partner is hyper-aroused or numb. You may also know that telling him he's hyperaroused or numb will probably only make his condition worse. If so, then there's no need to state the obvious. A caring look or a simple "I love you" or "How can I help?" might be better.

2. If at any point he looks bored or agitated, or starts shutting down or questioning your motives, quickly summarize your reflections and stop.

3. If your partner was ever held captive and interrogated, such as in a domestic violence situation or in a military or police matter, he may have problems with reflecting. One of the ways a power holder in these situations tries to intimidate his victims or force confessions out of them is by repeating or paraphrasing what they say over and over again. A power holder can also use reflection to try to trick victims into contradicting themselves. He can then accuse them of lying and use that as an excuse to abuse or torture them.

GIVING YOUR PARTNER A CHOICE

As always, it's important to give your partner reasonable choices. If he's depressed or struggling with some other problem, he may feel that dealing with your reflections, even of the facts of his message, might put him over the edge. So even if he doesn't seem to be that upset, you might want to ask, "Would you like to hear what I think you've been saying so you can tell me if I heard you correctly?"

Suppose he agrees to hear your reflections of what he said, but he hasn't said a word about his feelings. You may have some thoughts about how he might be feeling based on his body language. Once again, be sure to ask before you share your thoughts about his emotions: "Would you like to know what I think you might be feeling right now, and you can tell me if I'm way off base?" Even if you're sure he'd be interested, ask first.

SCREENING YOUR REFLECTION

Before you say anything, think about how what you're planning to say might sound to your partner. Leave out anything that might sound insulting or threatening. Also avoid any known trauma-related triggers, as well as the approaches you listed in your journal entry, "Ways I Communicate That Don't Work Well for My Partner."

WHEN TO PARAPHRASE

Sometimes it doesn't make any difference whether you reflect your partner's message by stating his exact words or by paraphrasing—using your own words. But given his PTSD, sometimes it does. It's usually fine to paraphrase when you're reflecting the factual parts of your partner's message. On the other hand, when you're reflecting an emotion that he stated he's having, it's generally best to use his exact words. Many survivors have had their feelings misinterpreted by others. If you paraphrase using a word with a somewhat different meaning, he may react negatively.

You may not know how to phrase something without it sounding critical or threatening. If so, then share your dilemma with him: "I'm stuck. You said something important, but I don't know how to reflect it back to you. I'm afraid it might sound offensive or bring up bad memories."

RESPONDING TO TRAUMATIC DETAILS

If your partner has just told you about parts of his trauma or another trauma, or about a death, losing a job promotion, or another loss or major frustration, there's usually no need to repeat the details of the story.

You can summarize his story in two or three sentences if you want. But it's more important to acknowledge the emotions and hardships involved in his story. You can do this in a few words, using statements such as "How sad," "So that's how it happened," "And you survived all that!" or "How unfair!" (See Step 3: Empathy for suggestions on showing compassion.)

PAYING ATTENTION TO BODY LANGUAGE

When Darnell came home, he walked slowly to the kitchen with a blank look on his face. He stood there for ten minutes without saying anything. Nina wondered if he was upset about something. Then he became irritated with her because of the way she had folded the kitchen towels. Now Nina knew that Darnell was unhappy about something fairly important, because usually he didn't care about how towels were folded. But since he didn't mention being upset, she didn't know whether or not to ask him about it.

What if your partner hasn't said a word about his emotions, but his body language is letting out signals that he's experiencing some strong feelings? Should you reflect what you're sensing?

Your decision will depend on your partner's personality. You'll also need to rely on your intuition. Some people crave being understood emotionally. Others don't like having their feelings exposed unless they choose to expose them. If your partner is usually uncomfortable showing or talking about his emotions, or, if at that particular moment, you sense that mentioning anything having to do with feelings would further upset him, then it's better not to risk it.

REFLECTING BODY LANGUAGE

If your partner is open to hearing your reflections on his mood, but hasn't talked about feeling a certain way, your reflections will be based on his body language. When you reflect, be sure to let him know that this is how you *think* he feels rather than how you *know* he feels.

You could say, for example, "I'm concerned about you. When you were telling me that story, you seemed to stammer a lot and your face looked flushed. You were breathing hard, too—at least that's how it looked to me. That makes me wonder if you're quite upset about it, or maybe about something else. Or maybe you aren't feeling well. I hope you're okay."

Notice how in these statements you'd be describing his body language as carefully and specifically as possible, but also in a caring manner. Then you'd be presenting your thoughts about what his physical cues mean as *your ideas*, rather than as *facts*. (Even if they are facts, he might not agree.) You would be clearly stating how *you* think he might be feeling. But you'd be leaving it up to *him* to define how he's feeling. ·

Remember that body language is not an exact science. Body language experts warn against jumping to conclusions based on one or two nonverbal cues. The only way you'll know for sure whether you're reading your partner's body language correctly is if you ask him for feedback later on (step 4: Getting It Right).

CHOICE POINTS

Step 2 involves many choice points. At various points in time, you'll be deciding whether to simply listen or to reflect (or ask to reflect) the factual or the emotional aspects of your partner's message, If you choose to reflect, you'll also be making decisions about how to do so. At such times you'll need to rely on your intuition, your past experience with him, and your own best judgment.

No hard-and-fast rules. You'll always need to screen your reflections for possibly triggering or offensive words and for ways of communicating that you know don't work. But other than that, there are no hard-and-fast rules.

For example, you were cautioned earlier against reflecting the details of your partner's trauma. You may discover, however, that he finds great comfort in that. You were also advised to not point out your partner's signs of hyperarousal or numbing. Yet for some survivors, it's a great relief to hear someone say, "You're breathing, talking, and moving so slowly, it seems like you're shutting down." Your partner may even be deeply moved by your caring enough to take such careful notice of his distress. Yet on another occasion, the exact same reflection could spark an argument or more numbing.

Judging your reflections. As you learn from experience, try not to judge the wisdom of your decisions by your partner's reactions. If your reflection (or your failure to reflect) upsets him, it doesn't necessarily mean that you made a mistake. If you made an honest effort to listen to him, be aware of his emotions, and reflect in a certain way (or not reflect) based on your understanding of his needs at the moment, congratulate yourself. That took a lot of hard work, self-control, and love. That's all that can be expected and, unfortunately, probably more than he'll receive from most others.

Learning from your partner's negative reactions. Try to view his negative reactions as a source of valuable information rather than as a sign of your failure. Every time he reacts negatively, you're learning about what he can and can't tolerate. Even if you carefully screened your reflection for known triggers, you might have been unaware of others. He himself may not have known about these triggers. It can take decades to uncover all of one's triggers! But as you both become aware of them, your entire relationship can improve.

Sometime later, you can talk to him about times you were confused about what to do, and ask for his input. At the very least, this approach will show him how carefully you've been trying to listen to him and how respectful you are of his needs.

You could say, for example, "I need to ask you something. I'm not trying to criticize you or call you illogical. I'm just confused and need your help so I can better understand.

"Here's what I'm confused about: Sometimes when I reflect back what I think you're feeling, you say that I'm treating you like a child or a wimp. But a couple of times when I didn't mention your emotions, you said I didn't care about your feelings.

"Who knows? Maybe I misunderstood, or you were talking about something else. If so, straighten me out. That's the whole point of this reflection business—making sure I hear you right."

The importance of reflection. Reflection can be a frustrating and tedious process. To complicate matters even further, your partner's reactions to certain types of reflection may change as he changes or grows. If, at some point, he decides to learn active listening and begins reflecting your words and feelings back to you, you might have negative reactions to step 2 as well.

Do not, however, abandon the idea of reflecting. It's a necessary step toward making sure you're understanding your partner and letting him know he's been heard. The skills involved in reflection are fundamental to all communication.

Step 3: Responding to Your Partner's Emotions

Many people think that the difference between happy and unhappy couples is that happy couples have found a way to resolve most of their differences. Relationship expert John Gottman (1999) says otherwise. According to his research, happy couples have just as many arguments as unhappy ones. The difference, he explains, is that happy couples have an emotional bank account that keeps them connected despite their conflicts.

Couples establish this emotional bank account of mutual affection and respect in three ways: by making an effort to remind themselves of what they cherish about each other, by empathizing with each other's difficulties, and by celebrating each other's joys (Gottman 1999).

You and your partner can do the same.

EMPATHY

The word empathy comes from the Greek word *empathos*, meaning being emotionally "with" the suffering and other feelings experienced by someone due to a mishap or misfortune. Empathy involves more than reflecting your partner's statements about her feeling; you need to put yourself in her place.

If you were your partner, what would you be thinking and feeling about the situation at hand? How would you be viewing yourself as a person? Would you be feeling proud or ashamed? Confused or confident? What might you be needing or wanting? What decisions might you be facing (Guerney 1989)? How might having PTSD influence your thoughts and feelings?

Recalling times when you were in a similar situation or had similar feelings may be able to help you empathize. For example, when Kitty rejected Paul's compliments, at first Paul felt angry and hurt.

Even after she told him about how her father would butter her up before attacking her, Paul still felt Kitty was overreacting and making excuses.

But then Paul remembered one of his supervisors. This supervisor would always tell him what a great worker he was, then hand him a poor evaluation. When Paul remembered how he felt misled and used by this supervisor, he was able to move past his hurt and feel compassion for Kitty.

In general, if your partner is hurting, it's best to keep the focus on her, not you. On the other hand, sometimes mentioning that you had a somewhat similar experience can let your partner know that you have some sense of what she's feeling.

Comparing pain. If you do refer to one of your experiences, be as brief as possible.

Also, be careful not to say, "I know how you feel." The truth is, you can't know exactly how she feels, just as she can't know exactly how you feel. If her experience was traumatic and yours wasn't, she may feel insulted by your comparing your pain to hers. So it's better to share your experience without comparison. If, for example, she's grieving the loss of a sibling to suicide, you could say, "I remember how sad, lonely, and lost I felt after my father died."

Also avoid comparing her pain with the sufferings of others. Saying or implying that your partner's pain is greater, lesser, or the same as somebody else's can lead to anger, guilt, or misunderstanding.

Expressing empathy. Nobody likes to be told how she feels, especially a survivor. So unless your partner has expressed certain thoughts and feelings, make it clear that your expressions of empathy are based on how you *think* she feels rather than on any definite knowledge. You can say, for example, "I'm wondering if you're feeling angry," or "You seem sad," or "Most people I know would be upset if they were in your shoes."

You can express empathy in a few words—such as "That's rough," "Bummer," "Too much!" "Terrible, just terrible," "So sad," "How unfair!" "I'm speechless," or "I bet that hurt"—or through caring expressions: "I wish it never happened," or "If only I could take away the pain." You can also show empathy without saying anything, by gently touching your partner or by listening without interrupting, nodding in agreement, or moving closer to her. If you aren't sure if she wants to be touched at that particular moment, ask, or simply say, "I feel like holding your hand," or "I'd like to give you a hug."

Be very careful to avoid any comments that are not empathic—comments such as "I told you so," "I would have been more careful," "Whining again?" "Others are worse off," or "Is it really that bad?" Also keep in mind that sometimes your partner may want help rather than empathy. You won't know until you ask: "Do you want help with this, or do you just want me to listen?" (Gottman 1999).

When your partner shuns empathy. In deciding how to respond, as always, screen whatever you plan to say or do for anything that might trigger or offend your partner. For example, Nina knew that if she said anything that sounded the least bit like empathy to Darnell, he'd view it as pity and be insulted. The best way to be empathic to Darnell, therefore, was just to listen intently.

Nina might also choose to say something like "This isn't pity and I don't feel sorry for you. I'm sure you'll handle things. But to me, your situation is very depressing." Or she could say, "Tough spot, but you're tough too," or "Sounds awful to me, but I've never known you to give up without a fight." Notice that she'd be commenting on how difficult Darnell's situation is without suggesting that he's weakened by it.

"Never again" is the slogan of some survivors. After having been victimized or overpowered once by a trauma, they promise themselves that they'll do everything in their power to make sure nothing ever overcomes or defeats them again. Hence when they find themselves in another situation where the cards are stacked against them, they may not want to face the fact that, once again, they're trapped.

The situation may not be traumatic. It could be, for example, a difficult work situation. But the problem isn't just that the work situation is difficult; it's that the person needs the job and wouldn't easily be able to find a new one. So he's stuck, just like he was stuck in the trauma, with no way out.

If your partner has this mind-set, your empathy for his situation could make him furious. Why? Because he doesn't want to be reminded that, once again, he's being oppressed and can't do much about it. On the other hand, at times he may find comfort in having someone acknowledge the oppressiveness of his situation and his resulting feelings of powerlessness.

Learning from experience. Not all survivors have this "never again" mind-set. There are some who depend on their partners' empathic understanding of their hardships to sustain them when they meet with another situation in which they don't have many choices.

Once again, you'll need to learn from experience what proves supportive. Don't be dismayed if you get it wrong sometimes. If you're trying to put yourself in your partner's place, the caring behind your effort will show.

Responding empathically when your partner is critical. Your partner doesn't have the right to be abusive. But she does have the right to complain about you, just as you have the right to complain about her. She also has the right to be grouchy, tired, and unreasonable. So do you.

But how can you possibly empathize with her if she's complaining about you? Doesn't that mean you're agreeing with her complaints? What if her complaints aren't abusive, but are petty or unfair?

Responding empathically to her complaints doesn't mean you're agreeing with them. You're only agreeing with her right to think or feel however she says she's thinking or feeling (provided she's not being abusive). When you empathically reflect your partner's criticisms, you're acting like a mirror. Her criticisms may be aimed at you, but you aren't accepting them or taking them in as truths about yourself. Instead you're reflecting them—turning them away from you and giving them back to her. And you're doing so in a nonaggressive way, which helps to preserve your relationship.

There's even reason to hope that after she hears enough of her complaints reflected back to her, she might realize how unreasonable or uncaring she's been. Sometimes people aren't aware of what they're actually saying when they're being unfair. But when they hear their words reflected back to them with empathy, at least they have the opportunity to see that maybe they overreacted or were unnecessarily harsh.

CELEBRATING THE POSITIVES

You can make "deposits" into your relationship's emotional bank account by being supportive of your partner and reacting with interest and enthusiasm to the good things that happen to her (Seligman 1991).

Suppose she learns that an army buddy she thought had been killed is still alive. Rejoice with her. Smile. Tell her how happy you are for her. Focus on her good news by asking questions about it: What's her buddy's name? Where did they serve together?

Happiness as a trigger. For some survivors, joy can be painful, because it highlights how depressed and pessimistic they usually feel. In other words, happiness is a trigger. Happiness means enjoying the moment. It requires letting your guard down and exposing yourself to possible danger. Did your partner's trauma occur while she was happy? Does she blame herself for being so relaxed or so busy having fun that she didn't notice an attacker or an enemy soldier? Then, for her, even being happy can be tainted.

If this is true for your partner, it doesn't mean that you have to stifle your expressions of joy. If anything, you need to show your partner that joy is possible—and safe. But don't be disappointed or blame yourself if she doesn't seem to be as excited or happy as you are about the good thing that happened to her. A sense of doom is a symptom of PTSD. This symptom varies in strength from one person to the next. But it's always there, lurking in the background, distracting the survivor from the goodness in her current life.

A survivor explains: "Before something bad happens to you, you know bad things happen in life, but you never think anything bad will happen to you. But after something bad happens to you, you're always waiting for it to happen again. You just can't trust anymore."

If you notice your partner's happiness starting to fade, don't comment on it. This is not the time for reflecting the change in her feelings or asking why she suddenly seems so down. Instead, gradually (not abruptly) back off from talking about her good news. But before you end the conversation, it's important to somehow affirm the positive. Quietly but warmly tell her again how glad you are that something good happened to her. And let her know that if she wants to celebrate, you're definitely available.

WHEN YOU CAN'T RESPOND EMPATHICALLY OR ENTHUSIASTICALLY

Undoubtedly there will be times when your partner is happy (or troubled) and you don't have the time or energy to react as you'd like. But you can at least acknowledge the importance of her message and say you're sorry that you can't give it the attention it deserves. Then promise to discuss it with her soon and—this is very important—make good on your promise.

For example, you could say, "That's such good (bad) news! I want to hear more about it, but unfortunately I can't right now. When can we talk?" Or, you could look her in the eyes, take her by the hand, and say, "I'm a little distracted right now, so it might not show, but I think that what happened to you is wonderful—really wonderful—and I'm very happy for you."

There may also be times when you're afraid your partner's positive experience could result in her having less time for you, or extra expenses, or some other undesirable consequence. You might be envious of her good fortune, and thus have mixed feelings about her happiness.

Depending on the nature of her positive event, you may even be so angry and resentful that you feel little or no joy for her whatsoever. For example, suppose you feel that this positive event would never have come to pass if it weren't for your sacrifices. Yet she's never shown much appreciation for the hard work you've been doing for her behind the scenes. Perhaps she even resisted your efforts to help her. But now she's enjoying the results of your labor.

You may then feel like bursting forth with a list of your concerns or resentments. It may be important to voice these concerns. But it would be better to bring them up at some later time. Allow your partner to enjoy the moment.

If you can't be happy for her, you can at least comment on the positive aspect of her news and ask for more information about what happened. This additional information could make you even more worried or angry. But you might also find out that some of your fears are unrealistic. She might even end up thanking you for your contributions to her positive experience.

Step 4: Getting It Right

Step 4 involves asking your partner for feedback regarding your reflections. There are many ways to phrase this request: "Did I hear you right? Tell me if I missed something," "Is that how you're feeling? I want to know if I heard you wrong or left out something important," or "Do you feel like I understood? If not, tell me where I'm off. I really want to know."

RESPONDING TO YOUR PARTNER'S CORRECTIONS

Accept his corrections even if you disagree. Perhaps you feel he's in denial about something. But if he's truly in denial, your insisting that he face a particular truth will only increase his resistance to accepting that truth. At some point you might want or need to confront him. But during active listening, the goal is to understand your partner as he needs to be understood at that moment.

WHEN YOUR PARTNER REJECTS
YOUR REFLECTIONS

Your partner may have had numerous experiences of being misunderstood by others, and he may easily become frustrated with you if he feels your reflections are incorrect. If so, then you can apply your active listening skills to his message of frustration. Pay full attention to what he's saying by maintaining eye contact and following the other suggestions listed under step 1. Then move on to step 2 and reflect back to him what he said or how he's feeling about what he sees as your mistakes—for example, "If I heard you right, you're upset with me because I misinterpreted your reaction."

Perhaps you tried hard to understand what your partner was saying. Perhaps he's the one who misunderstood your reflections because he didn't listen carefully, or because he was anxious or depressed. If so, it may be hard for you to stomach his complaints. But as long as he isn't being abusive, you will then proceed to step 3 and empathize with his feelings. To show compassion for his disappointment, you might say, for example, "I can see why you're irritated. I'd feel the same way if someone didn't hear me right about something so important." You'll then be back to step 4 (Getting It Right), focusing on making sure you understand him correctly.

Once he feels you understand his frustration with you, tell him you'd like to try again: "I want to be here for you in the way you need me to be. I can do that better if I have a better handle on what you're saying and feeling. How about I try again?"

Hopefully, active listening will become a habit, not a chore. At the very least, when you find yourself in the midst of a disagreement, you may want to backtrack to figure out whether you've misunderstood something. Following steps 1 through 4 will help ensure that you've heard him correctly.

If you suspect that your partner may have misunderstood some of the things that you have said, consider asking him to repeat some of your statements back to you, as well. You could say, for example, "Just to make sure we're on the same page, can you tell me what you remember me saying about that?"

ACTIVE LISTENING AS DEFUSING

In real life it's practically impossible to use active listening every time you talk to your partner. And active listening alone can't resolve all your relationship issues. But it can lay the groundwork for resolving these issues by helping to avoid preventable misunderstandings.

Active listening can also help defuse tense situations that could easily grow into major arguments, such as when you've just been criticized by your partner but it's not the right time or place to discuss the matter.

For example, the night Darnell came home from his trauma group, he complained to Nina about how she folded the towels, and then criticized how she'd set the table. Nina was ready to ask him why he was picking on her. But then she remembered that Darnell was usually out of sorts after group. She herself was tired from having fought traffic for an hour running an errand for Darnell.

Since both of them were in a negative frame of mind, Nina decided that discussing Darnell's unreasonable grouchiness could easily cause a major blowup. So she used active listening. "You're unhappy about the way the towels are folded and disappointed in me as a wife because I didn't set the table the way you liked," she reflected to him.

Yet this hurtful, tension-filled moment was the very time when it was very difficult for Nina to set aside her feelings and listen carefully, reflect, and empathize. (Most people need to be somewhat relaxed and emotionally calm to even remember steps 1 through 4, much less use them.)

When your partner starts complaining about you, quite naturally your first impulse may be to defend yourself or lash back with complaints of your own. This is especially the case if his criticisms are unfair and, even more so, if you happen to be tired, needing something from him, or frustrated in some other area of life. At such times it's understandable if, instead of using active listening, you become defensive and try to explain yourself in order to show your partner how unreasonable he's being. It's also understandable if you try to let him know how unhappy you are by becoming silent, withdrawing emotionally, or giving him a scowling look.

Responding in these ways, however, puts you in opposition to him. Defensiveness, emotional withdrawal, and other nonverbal forms of protest are not outwardly aggressive. Yet they are a type of attack. Why? Because they're telling your partner that you don't accept his right to think or feel whatever he's thinking or feeling. As long as he's not being abusive, he has the right to say what's on his mind, even if he's mistaken.

When you become defensive, perhaps you hope that he'll realize how wrong he's been and apologize. But instead, he's likely to feel attacked and feel that he needs to defend himself. Since his PTSD is the result of being attacked by something or someone, he's especially likely to feel attacked and need to defend himself.

While some survivors quickly go on the offensive, others immediately withdraw from any type of conflict. If your partner is a survivor of child abuse or domestic violence, he may instinctively withdraw from conflict as he did during his trauma. If he has military or police training, he may become silent or leave your presence because he knows he has the power to hurt you. Some veterans and police officers leave home for hours, if not days, until they're sure they won't become violent.

When you respond with active listening, you aren't resisting his complaint. You aren't giving him a reason to feel attacked or to need to defend himself by withdrawing, lashing out at you, or some other way.

On the surface, responding with active listening instead of telling him how you really feel may seem like you're passively allowing him to walk all over you. But there is nothing passive about active listening. You aren't doing nothing; you're doing something that requires an enormous amount of patience and self-control. Being able to consciously plan how to respond to a difficult situation while you're still in it, and still reacting to an unexpected emotional blow, is quite a feat!

WHEN NOT TO USE ACTIVE LISTENING

Active listening can help prevent a situation from becoming increasingly hostile. But sometimes you'll need to stand up for yourself, or leave the room. For instance, if Darnell had continued saying hurtful things to Nina, she may have needed to leave his presence.

Active listening is of limited use in situations in which the other person's intention is to inflict harm. Even if your partner isn't physically violent, if he berates you frequently or unfairly you will need to address his behavior in ways other than active listening.

Even if his criticisms aren't frequent, but are unfair, at some point you will need to bring this to his attention so it can be corrected. No matter how skilled you are at active listening or how strong you are as a person, being criticized at almost every turn will wear you down.

REALISTIC EXPECTATIONS

You may spend hours learning steps 1 to 4 and be extremely patient with your partner when using them. But just because you listen carefully and respond empathically to your partner doesn't automatically mean that he will listen carefully and be empathic toward you in return. For the active listening to go both ways, he will need to make an effort to learn how. Yet even if he doesn't make that effort, he'll learn some aspects of steps 1 to 4 by observing your use of the active listening skills.

Effective Self-Expression

Positive communication involves not only active listening, but effective self-expression. You can increase the probability that your partner will listen to and understand your thoughts and feelings by following a few key guidelines.

Be as Clear as Possible

Being clear is always important, but especially when speaking to someone whose ability to focus may be clouded by depression, painful memories, another PTSD symptom, or a trauma-related medical problem. If your partner's trauma was caused by or included confusing directions or statements that made the outcome worse, or if she was deliberately misled or manipulated by vague or mixed messages, ambiguity can be a trigger.

Ambiguous messages can lead to confusion, which is also a trigger in that confusion is part of every trauma. Trauma is so unexpected and overpowering that when it first occurs, there's confusion about whether or not it's really happening, followed by confusion about what actually *is* happening. Then there's confusion about what to do next.

Hence it's critical to be as clear and direct as possible, without speaking to her as if she were a child. This approach is not a reflection on your partner's intelligence. Almost anyone can become confused, anxious, or irritated when confronted with a complicated or indefinite message. But for survivors, confusion and ambiguity can have terrible associations. The smarter and more educated your partner is, the more likely she is to view her difficulty understanding you as proof that PTSD has made her "stupid." Then she'll feel inadequate and discouraged.

Some messages are complicated or inexact by nature, and you may have a hard time presenting a certain topic straightforwardly. If so, warn your partner: "This part sounds confusing, so bear with me."

Be Specific

Be as specific as possible about what you want, the problem at hand, or ways it could be solved. Avoid making global generalizations or using terms such as "always" or "never." If you're giving your partner feedback about her, focus on a specific behavior or specific situation, rather than on her as a person. For example, if you feel she's neglecting you, mention the specific ways you think she's neglecting you. Say, "You canceled our last five date nights," rather than "You're unreliable," or "You don't love me."

Avoid Overload

Many people feel overwhelmed when presented with a lot of information at the same time, but especially survivors. Presenting too much information or too many issues at once can recreate the sensory and information overload associated with trauma. During trauma, individuals are barraged with a great number of actions, objects, and details that need to be sorted out as thoroughly and quickly as possible in order ·to ensure survival. But because there are so many things going on, it can be difficult to figure out which ones are important and which ones are not.

When the situation is so confusing, it's easy to make mistakes. Although such mistakes are understandable, they can be the source of lifelong guilt, shame, and regret. As a result, when your partner feels confused by too much information, she may start to feel anxious or panicked, as if she is reexperiencing her trauma. She will then be less accessible to you.

When having serious conversations, limit your main points to three.

Own Your Feelings

Own your feelings by stating them as if they matter, and by expressing them directly.

An emotion can be expressed directly by naming it ("I'm furious"), by using a figure of speech ("I feel like a volcano inside"), or by describing its effect on you ("I'm so angry I'm thinking of leaving you" or "I'm wondering if you're cheating on me").

Indirect ways of communicating feelings don't work as well as direct ways because they don't specify your exact feeling. Examples of indirect of ways of expressing feelings include name-calling ("You liar"), sarcasm ("Do you neglect your mother too?"), asking questions ("Are you having an affair?"), issuing commands ("Don't touch me!"), and hurling accusations ("You did that on purpose.").

Directly expressing love or admiration requires being specific, as well. For example, a direct way of saying "You're terrific" might be "I appreciate how tenderly you touch me," or "Sometimes just looking at you makes me so happy I could cry."

Avoid the Word "Should"

Speak in terms of wishes, desires, needs, or specific feelings, instead of "shoulds." For example, say, "I miss our date nights. I need that time with you," rather than "You should be more considerate and keep your promises."

Be as Positive as Possible

Whenever it's relevant, mention your positive feelings and intentions toward your partner, her positive qualities and contributions, and any positive memories related to the topic or situation at hand. If you dislike something she's doing, point out any possible positive reasons she may have for doing what she's doing. Also mention the good feelings you had (about her, yourself, your life, or your relationship) when that behavior didn't exist, or that you think you'll have once it has stopped (Guerney 1987).

Share Your Concerns

Describe your concern, then state your purpose: "I hesitate to mention this, because I haven't thought it out yet. It might sound as if I'm criticizing you, but that's not my purpose. My goal is to share my concern."

Preface Potential Sore Points

Use phrases such as "in my opinion" and "as I see it" to introduce any thoughts or feelings that your partner may disagree with (Guerney 1987).

Electronic Communication

Emailing and texting are fine for communicating about routine matters, but not as useful for addressing emotional ones. All of the information that can be gained from a person's voice and facial expressions are lost. In fact, the entire message could be lost due to technological failure, or could accidentally be forwarded to others.

Unless electronic messaging is the only means of communication available, it's best saved for sharing information or simple, positive emotions such as love or joy, rather than settling disputes. To avoid unnecessary hurt feelings and misunderstandings, come to some agreement with your partner about how quickly you expect one another to respond to each other's emails, texts, or calls.

Additional Ways to Avoid Conflicts

You may know your partner quite well, but you aren't a mind reader. Neither is she. Especially during times of stress, it's easy to misinterpret each other's silences, gestures, facial expressions, and tone of voice as personal rejections or criticisms. These misunderstandings can lead to unnecessary flare-ups and resentments. Some of these needless conflicts can be avoided by using reality checks and letting your partner know when your mood or behavior isn't her fault. Perhaps she can do the same.

Reality Checks

Reality checks are ways of finding out if what you think your partner is thinking or feeling is actually what's she's thinking or feeling. For example, if she looks sullen and you recently had a disagreement, you might legitimately wonder if she's still upset with you. You might be right, but she could be troubled by something else. You needn't increase her stress by asking her to explain her mood. But you don't have to waste your psychic energy wondering if you're somehow responsible and then feeling angry, hurt, guilty, or anxious, when you may have had little or nothing to do with her mood.

Instead, you could do a reality check by saying, "I need to check something out with you. Maybe I'm off base, but I'm wondering if you're upset with me because of ..." and then mentioning the specifics. "I'm not trying to start an argument or a long discussion. If you're miffed with me, we don't have to talk about it. All I need is a yes-or-no answer so I can know if I'm reading you right."

Letting Your Partner Know When It's Not Her Fault

Similarly, if you're in a bad mood, you can spare your partner from wondering if your mood is related to her by making a short statement such as "I'm feeling down right now. I don't need to talk about it. Just know it's not about you." You could also use a prearranged hand signal or object to communicate this message. For example, you could cross your fingers, blow on a finger, blow her a kiss, scribble on (or turn over) a piece of paper, turn a small article of clothing inside out, or make a circle with your thumb and index finger.

Like all methods of communication, reality checks and letting your partner know something is not her fault are most effective if they're not overused.

EXERCISE 3.3: Applying Positive Communication Skills

Earlier in this chapter you completed exercise 3.1: "Learning from the Past." In number 3 of that exercise you wrote about times you and your partner had problems communicating. In the following exercise you'll return to those instances of unsuccessful communication and see how using the communication skills you've learned in this chapter could have helped those talks go more smoothly.

Select one of those instances and answer the following questions:

1. When could you have used active listening skills, such as attentive listening, reflection, or empathy, during this conversation? Would having used one or more of these skills have helped? If so, how? Write out what you would have said using these skills.

2. If you'd known about the guidelines for effective self-expression, how would you have expressed yourself differently? How would following these guidelines have affected the outcome of your talk? Write out how you could have expressed certain thoughts and feelings more effectively.

3. Were there times when you missed a chance to reward your partner for speaking in helpful ways, or to show him how to talk to you in ways that work for you? How would you have rewarded him or instructed him? Write out what you would have said.

4. How could you have celebrated your partner's positive mood or experiences? Write out what you would have done.

5. Are there any other ways you could have communicated differently with your partner that would have made a positive difference? For example, were there times you could have been more clear or specific? Write out what you would have said or done differently.

6. Answer the above questions for as many other instances of unsuccessful communication as you wish.

Perhaps the hardest time to remember to use active listening skills, positive self-expression skills, and techniques such as reality checks is when you're frustrated with your partner or when life just seems too hard for other reasons. At such times, most of us don't have the energy or patience to use a positive skill and can easily blurt out something we regret later.

In the following exercise, you'll try to apply some of the skills you've learned in this chapter to instances where either you or your partner resorted to name-calling or another communication pitfall. By imagining how you (or your partner) could have used a positive communication skill, you'll be more likely to use this skill in the future instead of falling into another communication pitfall.

EXERCISE 3.4: Avoiding Communication Pitfalls

In exercise 3.2: "Communication Pitfalls," you described times when your talks with your partner were scarred by a pitfall such as shaming or verbal abuse. Select one of the instances you described in number 2 and write a few sentences about how you could have used a positive communication skill to say what you wanted to say without being destructive.

Then select one of the instances you described in number 5 and write about how your partner could have used a positive communication skill instead of being negative.

You can repeat this process for the rest of the instances you listed in numbers 2 and 5.

In this chapter you learned how to listen and express yourself more effectively, and how to avoid certain communication pitfalls. You also examined the past to find the ways of communicating that work better than others. Then you applied the skills and techniques you learned to some of your communication problems.

In the next chapter, you'll learn how to apply the communication skills described in this chapter to the difficult problem of talking about your conflicts and other sensitive relationship issues. You'll also learn some ways of approaching your partner to ask for improvements in your relationship.

If you and your partner can face your disagreements without damaging your relationship, you may find that facing them can actually bring you closer together.

CHAPTER 4

Talking About Difficult Subjects and Making Decisions Together

Conflict is normal. Having relationship conflicts doesn't mean that you, your partner, or your relationship is a failure. In fact, facing your conflicts can make your relationship stronger if you approach these conflicts in ways that will improve your relationship rather than harm it.

This chapter explains how your partner's trauma could be affecting his ability to make decisions and discuss relationship problems. It provides guidelines that can help decision making and talking about difficult subjects go more smoothly. It also describes some of the dilemmas you might face when you ask for improvements in your relationship, as well as the steps you can take to help your ideas for change be as well received as possible.

Avoidance

Some of your disagreements may be related to your partner's PTSD, but others stem from deeply rooted personality or other differences. These personality differences would be creating problems in your relationship even if your partner didn't have PTSD.

Some conflicts are small and can be safely overlooked. But others are major and prevent couples from enjoying their relationship and making necessary decisions. One way to deal with these problems is to ignore them and hope they go away on their own. Some may actually lessen over time. But those that don't and aren't handled adequately can show up as explosions over trivia, snide remarks, frequent grumbling, sexual disinterest, or avoiding each other.

Ideally, couples talk about their differences and try to reach some type of compromise. But a general tendency is to avoid such discussions. A common fear is that these discussions could lead to a big fight, hurt feelings, or a standoff. Such discussions can also bring up memories of previous confrontations, either with one's partner or with someone else, that didn't go well. When these talks involve making an important decision, they can also raise anxiety about the future. And often, they present dilemmas, such as whether or not to compromise, or how to compromise without giving up too much of what one wants.

Relationship conflicts can trigger any number of traumatic memories and emotions for your partner. Trauma is the ultimate conflict, and it increases the normal tension involved in discussing relationship issues and making joint decisions.

Obstacles to Decision Making

Sometimes the experience of trauma causes people to see situations more clearly and sharpens their decision-making skills. But trauma can also distort survivors' attitudes toward decisions and negatively affect how they make them. In some homes the very process of making a decision can become a source of tension. It's hard enough for any two people who love each other to face their differences and try to reach agreements. But partners of survivors can also find themselves distressed by the way their mates go about making decisions—or not making them.

Most couples argue over decisions about time, money, sex, in-laws, and child-rearing. But survivors can have especially intense feelings about certain issues because of their trauma. For example, some survivors of violence want nothing to do with child discipline because they view all forms of discipline as abusive. Others may want to recreate the strict discipline they were raised with or were taught in the military or police force. When a partner doesn't agree, the survivor may be unwilling to bend, or may begin having more severe PTSD symptoms.

Decisions that involve trusting others, such as choosing a car mechanic or a babysitter, can be especially heated due to the survivor's trust issues. For example, Kitty spent ten hours on the phone checking out the facts about an item she wanted to purchase, whereas Paul was satisfied after five or six inquiries. Although having PTSD is associated with mistrust, some survivors vary between being extremely naive and being extremely cynical. This inconsistency can create confusion for the partner.

Decisions involving social activities can be especially difficult. Some survivors feel "invaded" and overwhelmed by having visitors in their home, no matter who the visitors are. Others tax the patience of their partners by offering hospitality, lodging, and money to fellow survivors without considering the effects on their partners.

Survivors Who Avoid Making Decisions

Because of his traumatic experiences, your partner may avoid making decisions for any number of reasons.

SELF-DOUBT AND FEAR OF RESPONSIBILITY

If your partner feels that a decision he made during his trauma contributed to a terrible event or chain of events, he may doubt his ability to make good decisions. Whether or not the decision he made during his trauma actually did lead to some type of disaster doesn't matter. If he believes that it did, he may fear that any decision he makes in his current life could also have a catastrophic outcome.

In this case, he might prefer that you make the decisions. That way, if something bad happens it won't be his fault, but yours.

Darnell explains: "I don't want to take responsibility for any more decisions! Overseas every decision I made, even a small one, could end up meaning someone's head got blown off. Now I'm afraid that if I pick the wrong school for my kids, something bad will happen to them. So I let Nina decide."

LOW SELF-ESTEEM AND GUILT

Your partner may also bow out of making decisions because he feels inferior or damaged due to his PTSD, or because he suffers from survivor guilt. If he feels he's failing you because of his trauma-related problems, he may try to make it up to you by letting you make certain decisions.

If he grew up in an abusive home or was in an abusive relationship, he may have been told that he didn't deserve to have his needs met and that his opinions were worthless. As a result, on some level he may expect that you won't really listen to him because he doesn't deserve to be heard. If he was abused as a child, he may have trouble identifying his needs. Perhaps he was never taught how to put them into words. Consequently he may avoid talking to you about decisions or want you to make them.

FEELINGS OF POWERLESSNESS

During trauma people are forced to submit to an overpowering person or force. Afterward some survivors carry the sense of powerlessness they had during their trauma into situations where they do have choices.

If your partner was abused as a child or was in an abusive relationship, she may not have been allowed to have a say in decisions. Or perhaps she (or someone else, or a pet) was made to pay if she didn't automatically agree with whoever was ruling the family by force. In her past, small disagreements usually led to violence. She may therefore hesitate to get involved in any kind of debate or decision making with you, even about minor matters.

Like some veterans and law enforcement officers, she may also be weary of conflict. She doesn't want any more struggles, especially at home. All she wants is peace.

In order to avoid a possible argument, she may tend to go along with what you want. She may even want you to handle certain decisions without consulting her first.

EFFECTS ON PARTNERS

If your partner avoids making decisions or looks to you to make them, you will have some degree of power in your relationship. But you may resent not having a partner who helps shoulder the burden of making decisions and the responsibility for their outcome.

You may often get your way. But your partner may agree with you in a half-hearted manner that is unsatisfying to you.

Survivors Who Need to Control Decisions

Because they had so little control during their trauma, some survivors are determined to control as many aspects of their current life as possible. Hence they may want to make most or all of the decisions at home.

Some formerly abused people don't know how to be, or aren't comfortable being, assertive. But others insist on having their own way. In their experience, most conflicts were resolved by intimidation and force rather than by negotiation and compromise. Unless they've had the benefit of counseling or a relationship-enhancement course, they may not know how to stand up for themselves without stepping on their partners' feelings. When they express their needs, they may do so in an overly demanding way.

Survivors with military training may be used to issuing orders, and expect their partners to obey them as if they were military commands. As soldiers, they were also trained to not give up without a fight. As a result, some may view compromise as a form of cowardice and stubbornly refuse to consider their partners' suggestions.

SENSE OF URGENCY

Some survivors don't necessarily want to dominate their partners or make all the decisions. Yet they end up taking over decisions because of their strong sense of urgency.

During their trauma they may have learned that delays in making decisions could have disastrous results. So they feel that all or most decisions need to be made right away. Yet some decisions can wait, and sometimes it's better to take some time to think things over and get more information.

When their partners object to making an immediate decision, arguments can result. In some cases, a survivor's sense of urgency is so strong that he makes a decision and acts on it against his partner's wishes. He may know that his partner wants to take more time to decide, but he doesn't even consult her first. He may feel justified, as if he's saving lives. But his actions create deep rifts in his relationship.

EFFECTS ON PARTNERS

If your partner wants to control most of the decisions, there may be power struggles in your relationship. Or you may feel oppressed or in a one-down position because he doesn't like to compromise. At times you can become so tired of standing up for yourself that you simply let him have the control he wants.

Survivors Who Take Forever to Make Decisions

If your partner feels she made a poor decision during her trauma, she may need to examine every aspect of a decision in great detail to be sure she doesn't make another mistake. But doing so can drag out the decision-making process and tax your patience.

"We can't get things done because Kitty puts every decision under a microscope," complains Paul. "But if I try to speed things up, she goes into a panic. The way she acts, you'd think the world might come to an end if we get the wrong color sofa."

Paul has come to understand that Kitty feels this way because her world did come to an end in the past—many times. "Everything has to be perfect now because everything was so bad in the past," he sighs. Yet he gets so frustrated with her perfectionism that he ends up leaving many decisions up to her.

Your partner may also take a long time to make a decision if she suffers from depression, chronic pain, or another trauma-related medical problem. She isn't necessarily avoiding decision making. But her condition may make it hard for her to concentrate on the issue at hand.

Her inability to decide leaves you hanging. You may also feel trapped. On the one hand, you want to settle the matter yourself and get it off your plate. On the other hand, you respect her right to have a say. Or perhaps you don't want her to feel more dependent and helpless than she already feels because of her medical or psychiatric problem. Also, if you make the decision without her, she may feel you're punishing her for problems that aren't her fault and accuse you of being unsupportive. Then both of you are likely to feel guilty and resentful at the same time.

Survivors Who Vary

Your partner's approach can vary greatly. Sometimes she avoids decisions as if they were the plague. Yet other times she demands that you agree with what she wants. During a discussion, she may suddenly become argumentative. But a few minutes later, she's almost tongue-tied and goes along with whatever you say.

People don't always act the same way in similar situations. It's also normal for people to change their minds in midstream. However some of your partner's variations may be PTSD-related.

Say, for example, you're having a discussion about a certain decision that, from your point of view, is going quite well. Although you disagree on a few minor points, there doesn't seem to be that much tension between you. So when she has an anxiety attack, becomes hostile, or starts shutting down, you're confused.

Because your partner was traumatized, it takes less tension and stress to set her off into high anxiety than it would a nontraumatized person. If her anxiety increases, it could lead to anger, and then possibly to a shutdown. Going from high anxiety to anger to numbing is a normal part of the PTSD cycle.

Your partner may also vary because of what the decision is about. She may have a sense of urgency about some issues but not others. She may avoid some kinds of decisions but want to dominate others.

Darnell's fear of responsibility, for example, causes him to leave most decisions up to Nina. But when Darnell smells danger, he springs into action. Nina may think he's overreacting. But when he feels that something is a matter of life or death, he's unstoppable.

How to Make Decisions and Talk About Difficult Subjects

Despite the many obstacles described above, there are ways of discussing joint decisions and difficult subjects that can make both you and your partner feel safer and more comfortable.

This section provides two sets of guidelines that can help make such discussions more productive: "Getting Ready for Your Discussion" and "Discussion Guidelines." Follow only those guidelines that you think would be helpful.

Getting Ready for Your Discussion

A few days before you talk to your partner, prepare for your discussion by following the guidelines provided below.

1. Set a specific time and place for your discussion. Pick a place where you both feel comfortable and can't be easily distracted.

2. Decide on a time limit for your discussion. Agree that whenever one of you can't pay enough attention to the topic, you'll stop and plan another time to meet.

    During his trauma, your partner had no idea of when it would end and no way out. Putting time limits on your talk and having a way out in case your meeting becomes too uncomfortable makes these discussions less stressful.

3. Agree to stick to your agenda.

4. Prioritize your problems and divide large problems into smaller parts. Work on one part at a time.

5. Focus on solvable problems (or parts of problems). Making headway on solvable issues is better for your relationship than becoming frustrated trying to solve unsolvable ones. And success in solving some of the issues can reduce tensions caused by the unsolvable ones.

6. Agree that if you're discussing finances, you won't bring up other problems, such as in-laws.

7. If you need more information before you meet in order to make a good decision, agree on how this work will be divided between you.

   Some survivors, especially those with depression, view tasks as being harder than they really are. If your partner has this problem, discuss what's involved in getting the job done. For example, if the task is collecting information, discuss where he can find it, who or what can help him, and how long it will take. Break the task down into a series of small steps.

8. Establish ground rules about what's acceptable behavior and what isn't. In counseling couples, Guerney (1987) has each partner answer these questions: "What's acceptable for me to do or say during/after our meeting?" and "What's acceptable for my partner to do or say during/after our meeting?"

   Physical violence and communication pitfalls such as verbal abuse and cursing are clearly off limits. But you may also want to cover areas such as tone of voice and comments that are so hurtful they could make you (or your partner) feel like lashing out or leaving the room. Also discuss ways you might try to punish each other after your talk for something that was said. Punishment might include, for example, withholding sex or refusing to do certain chores.

9. Come up with agreed-upon ways to remind each other about the ground rules. For example, if one of you says something that's off limits, the other can say, "As I remember it, we agreed not to do that." Or you can create a hand signal as a reminder (Guerney 1987).

10. Agree that if one of you becomes increasingly angry, tense, or out of control, either of you can call a time-out.

    A time-out isn't a cop-out. It's a prearranged way of avoiding uncontrolled outbreaks of anger. Consider using a hand signal (such as a peace sign, or your hand on top of your head or over your heart), a small, safe object (such as a piece of paper or paper cup to turn over), or some other nonverbal way to call a time-out. Telling your partner that you're angry (or that he is) could trigger more anger.

    Time-outs need to be at least thirty minutes long, or enough time to calm down. You and your partner can agree on a specific time limit and time to reunite. You need to agree to stay on the premises, to not use alcohol or drugs or engage in any other type of self-destructive activity, to not harm property or any living thing, and to use the time apart to cool down.

    Some therapists ask clients to sign time-out contracts, which list all the necessary conditions for a time-out. You and your partner can write up your own time-out contract if you wish. If not, then you can show him this description of time-outs. If he won't agree to the necessary conditions of a time-out, all you can do is say that you plan to stick to the conditions.

11. Do your homework. Before you meet, write out your views or ideas as clearly and specifically as possible. Eliminate any potentially triggering or offensive words or phrases. If the topic involves a major conflict or a sensitive relationship issue,

you will need to take the steps outlined in the next section, "Asking for Change," in order to present your ideas effectively. Hopefully your partner will be willing to do the same.

All of the above guidelines apply regardless of the kind of problem you're trying to solve with your partner. If your partner tends to be controlling, pay special attention to suggestions 3, 6, and 8 through 11; if he tends to be passive, focus on suggestions 7 through 11.

Discussion Guidelines

On the day of and during your discussion, consider the following suggestions:

1. Before your meeting, take some time to relax.

2. If one of you is upset or sick, reschedule your meeting, unless it's urgent.

3. Use active listening, positive self-expression skills, reality checks, and other communication skills as needed. (See chapter 3.)

4. Periodically ask, "How's this going for you?"

5. Take stretch breaks and breathing breaks. The simplest kind of breathing break involves taking three deep breaths. Be sure to breathe in and out slowly. You can also take slow breaths in through the nose to a count of five, and then exhale through the mouth to a count of ten. Ask your partner to join you, if you wish.

6. If you feel that a certain matter isn't as urgent as your partner thinks it is, ask questions such as "When would be the ideal time to do it?" "What would be the absolute latest time?" "What will happen if we haven't done it by then?" "Do we

have enough information to set a deadline?" or "How long can you stand waiting?"

7. Talk about which decisions are reversible and which are not. Whenever possible, try to come up with short-term or experimental solutions, rather than permanent ones.

8. If you aren't making progress on a particular topic, agree to table it and discuss it at some later time.

9. When necessary, call for a time-out. Follow the instructions provided in number 10 of "Getting Ready for Your Discussion," above.

10. Make your solution as specific as possible. Be sure that it's realistic in terms of your time, finances, and other limitations.

11. As you get close to an agreement, ask your partner if it feels fair to him. Ask yourself the same question. Any decision you make needs to feel fair (or fair enough) to both of you. Otherwise it won't work (Guerney 1987).

12. Think about situations in which your solution might not work and include those in your agreement. Then set up a time to talk about how well your solution is working and to make any needed changes.

13. If your partner clearly indicates that he's reached his limit, feels like exploding, or has started to shut down, stop the meeting. Don't push yourself past your limits, either.

The above suggestions can be useful regardless of how your partner handles talking about difficult subjects. If he tends to avoid making decisions, pay special attention to suggestions 5 and 7 through 12; if he wants to control decisions, focus on suggestions 5, 7, and 9 through 13; and if he has a sense of urgency or is a perfectionist, note suggestions 6 through 8 and 11.

Asking for Change and Other Sensitive Relationship Issues

Sharing your complaints with your partner and asking for improvements in your relationship can be especially difficult. She may already feel inadequate or humiliated because of her trauma. She could easily feel so wounded or offended by your complaints that she may not even want to listen to you. Also, because of her PTSD, even positive changes can feel threatening to her.

Hence your approach needs to be as nonblaming as possible. An approach such as "Here's what's wrong with you; now fix it" will get you nowhere. You'll need to have a more productive attitude, such as this: "Because I know you love me, I know you don't want to see me in so much pain. I'm sure we can work together to help lessen my hurt. I have some ideas about what you could do to that would help me and that might benefit you as well. I'm willing to do my share, too, to make things better between us."

If you're angry with your partner, such an ideal attitude may seem impossible, if not hypocritical. You're definitely entitled to your anger! Yet it's possible to have angry feelings and still shift toward this more productive approach. Making such a shift, however, means you will need to do more than make a quick list of your complaints and the changes you want.

First, you'll need to face your feelings about your partner's problem behavior. Then you'll need to take stock of the problem situation and come up with some possible solutions. After deciding which solutions are realistic, you'll need to figure out the best way of presenting your ideas to your partner.

The suggestions and exercises in this section can help you confront your partner in the most nonthreatening and positive way possible. But working through this section can be both time consuming and emotionally draining. You'll probably need to start several weeks before meeting with her. You may also need to turn to a therapist or trusted friends for support and suggestions.

As you proceed through this section, you may find yourself resenting all the effort involved. Unfortunately there are no shortcuts. Relationship issues are always complicated. The more thought you put into what you're going to say and how you're going to say it, the greater the chances that your message will be heard.

Yet following the suggestions and completing the exercises provided below do not guarantee that you will see the changes you want in your relationship. Despite all your efforts, you may achieve little, and you may not know until months later if your actions had any real effect on your partner. But you will have the satisfaction of knowing that you made your best effort to improve matters.

Throughout your discussion, remember to follow the discussion guidelines provided earlier.

Facing Feelings

The purpose of presenting your complaint to your partner is to let her know why you want certain changes, not to blast her with all your anger and frustration. You can certainly tell her that you're angry with her. But releasing the full force of your anger, disgust, and other negative emotions in her presence will not bring about the change you desire (unless your goal is to alienate her).

Your raw negative feelings do need to be released, but in a way that doesn't harm anyone, or your relationship. If you need to vent, then vent to your therapist, friends, or trusted others. Scream or yell when you're alone, in your car, or somewhere where your venting won't hurt anyone. You can also write about these feelings, speak them into an audio recorder, or draw a picture of them. Then discard the paper, audio file, or picture.

Expressing your anger in one of these safe ways won't get rid of all of it. You'll probably still have some anger toward your partner when you meet with her. But hopefully you'll have released enough of your hostility beforehand that you don't explode at her during your talk.

EXERCISE 4.1: Writing a Letter to Your Partner

Perhaps one of the best ways to release your strong negative emotions toward your partner is to write a letter to her about her problem behavior. But don't give her the letter. The letter is for you, not her. Keeping it to yourself gives you the freedom to write down whatever you want.

Select a relationship problem to write about. You may have several pressing relationship problems. But when you meet with your partner, you need to discuss only one of them. Bringing up more than one complaint or other sensitive issue at the same sitting could overwhelm not only your partner, but also you.

In chapter 2, you wrote about some of your relationship issues in exercise 2.4 (Recognizing My Resentments and Disappointments) and 2.5 (Establishing Positive Goals for My Relationship). Your letter can be about one of these issues, or you can chose to write about a different one. If you're anxious about confronting your partner or have never confronted her before, you might want to start out with the smallest problem or with one you think would be the easiest for the two of you to handle.

On a separate page in your journal, entitled "Letter to My Partner," use the suggestions provided below to write a letter to your partner about the relationship problem you selected.

Be sure to observe the cautions described in the "Cautions" section in the introduction to this book. If writing this letter brings up traumatic or overwhelmingly painful memories, don't proceed without the permission of a qualified, licensed mental health professional.

Identify specifics. Describe the incidents that have led up to your complaint. What did she actually do or say that is now causing you so much distress? Be as specific as possible. You'll need to mention some of these specifics when you meet with her.

Express your negative feelings. As you describe these incidents, write down your negative feelings about your partner's behavior. If you aren't comfortable admitting to feeling hateful, jealous, or vengeful, this may be difficult for you. But putting your emotions on paper doesn't hurt anyone. As long as you don't show your letter to your partner, you're actually helping her and your relationship.

Think about hurts caused by others. As you're writing, you might start remembering others who wronged or cheated you. Write about what these people did to you and your resentments toward them. If other negative life events come to mind, write about those too.

If you don't have any such memories while writing this letter, ask yourself this question: Has anyone or anything in your life ever made you feel the same way (fed up, hurt, disgusted, and so forth) as you do about your partner's problem behavior? If so, write a few sentences about these individuals or events and your feelings toward them.

Uncover your sense of loss. When you first start writing, you may be bursting with anger and frustration. But if you write long enough and in enough detail, you'll probably start feeling sad, as well. Underneath your anger, contempt, and other negative emotions, there may be a sense of loss about not having gotten what you wanted, needed, or deserved from your partner or from others. If so, write about those losses and the grief that goes with them.

Take breaks. If this is the first time you've written such a letter, you may be overflowing with unexpressed emotions and wishes. You may therefore need to write it in stages and take frequent breaks. Even if you've completed a similar exercise before, you may be surprised at how much you have to say and how long it takes you to write it all down.

But however long it takes, it is time well spent. Releasing some of your strong negative emotions will help you think more clearly about what you want from your partner and how to approach her.

Sorting Out Feelings

Writing this letter can also help you sort out how much of your anger and pain is related to your partner's behavior and how much is the result of other people's misbehavior or other negative events. You'll then have a more realistic view of the causes of your unhappiness.

Like many partners, Nina longed for a closer relationship with her mate. Her list of specific incidents that made her feel shut out of Darnell's life included this: "During the last four months, Darnell canceled over half of our date nights at the last minute. He spends whole weekends helping his mother and his war buddies, but doesn't have one night a month for our relationship. When we go to family events, he says less than ten words to me."

As Nina wrote about these and similar incidents, she remembered others who had made her feel unimportant. While describing how much these other people had hurt and angered her, she realized something important. She became aware that one reason she was having such a deep negative reaction to Darnell's hurtful behavior was that others had treated her similarly in the past.

It's not that she was "overreacting" to Darnell's behavior. Even if she'd never felt rejected by others, Darnell's behavior would have been painful for her. Yet as a result of writing about how others had mistreated her, her anger at Darnell lessened. She was still furious with him. But now her anger toward him wasn't mixed in with her anger toward others who had mistreated her. Now it reflected his behavior, not the behavior of others.

EXERCISE 4.2: Sorting Out My Feelings

After you finish your letter, review it. Circle those incidents that have to do with your partner rather than other people or events. On a separate page in your journal, entitled "Sorting Out My Feelings," do some writing about how the uncircled incidents may be affecting your feelings toward your partner's problem behavior.

Taking Stock

So far you've described the incidents leading up to your complaint, and expressed and sorted out some of your feelings about these incidents. But when you meet with your partner, you'll need to be selective about which of these incidents you mention.

The following exercise can help you take stock of these incidents. You can then better decide which of them, or which parts of them, will most clearly show him what you're complaining about and why there's a need for change. You'll also need to take stock of your own behavior during these incidents.

EXERCISE 4.3: Taking Stock

On a separate page in your journal, entitled "Taking Stock," answer the following questions.

1. Of all the incidents you circled, those having to do with your partner, which ones are not discussable at this time?

2. Of the circled incidents that are discussable, which three caused you the most grief?

3. Review your descriptions of these three critical incidents in your letter. If you haven't done so already, pinpoint exactly what caused you the most pain or anger during these incidents.

4. Looking back, can you see any ways, however small, that you might have contributed to your relationship problem during these incidents? For example, Nina realized that one reason Darnell freely canceled so many of their dates was that she had never really told him how much it upset her when he did this.

5. Write out the three incidents (or particular moments in these incidents) that caused you the most pain, and your feelings about them, using the positive communication skills described in chapter 3. Acknowledge anything you might have done, however small, that might have helped create the problem or made it worse.

Designing and Assessing Possible Solutions

When you meet with your partner, present him with as many solutions as possible. Your solutions need to be specific and concrete.

EXERCISE 4.4: Possible Solutions

On a separate page in your journal, entitled "Possible Solutions," answer the following questions. As you do, take into account your partner's needs as well as your own.

1. Exactly what could your partner do differently that would help solve the problem? Come up with as many ideas as possible. Eliminate any solutions that would be unrealistic given your personalities, your partner's PTSD, and your life circumstances.

2. For each solution you think is realistic, answer the following questions: What would your partner be giving up? What would he be gaining? Are there any ways you can help him do whatever you're asking him to do? What are you willing to give up to help make this solution a reality? What would you be gaining in return?

3. Review your descriptions of the costs and benefits of various solutions you made in number 2, above. Based on your review, which two or three of these solutions would be the most desirable to you? Which two or three would be the least preferable? If you don't have that many solutions, then identify the solution you like the best and the one you like the least.

Identifying the Positives

"Darnell always has a good excuse for canceling our dates," Nina had written angrily at the beginning of her letter. "Either he has to work late or one of his relatives or war buddies needs him. I can understand having to work late. But when he makes time for them, but not for me, I hit the roof!"

Yet as she wrote about how angry she was with Darnell and how jealous she was of his relatives and friends, she realized what a loyal person Darnell was. The sense of duty that made him cancel their dinner dates was the same sense of duty that made him drop everything and be there for her whenever she really needed him.

She also became aware that one reason she was so angry about his cancelations was that she missed him, and she missed him because she loved him. Perhaps this seems obvious. But in her anger, Nina had lost sight of her positive feelings toward Darnell.

As you wrote about your anger toward your partner, perhaps you, like Nina, also realized how much you care about him and remembered the qualities you appreciate in him. Recognizing possible positive reasons your partner might have had for his problem behavior is not the same as making excuses for him. You're simply looking at his behavior from his point of view and giving him the benefit of the doubt. If you're mistaken, you'll find out soon enough.

EXERCISE 4.5: The Positives

On a separate page in your journal, entitled "The Positives," answer the following questions.

1. What positive feelings do you have toward your partner related to his problem behavior or the relationship problem troubling you?

2. What positive qualities or motivations might your partner have that are relevant to his problem behavior?

3. You need to mention your positive feelings, as well as your partner's positive qualities and possible positive motivations (identified in number 1 and number 2, above) when you confront him. Write out how you could include these positives in your complaint.

Originally Nina had planned to tell Darnell, "You say you love me, but you don't mean it," or "You treat me like a nothing." But after identifying the positives, she decided to say, "Darnell, I know you love me. I'll never forget how you took care of me after my surgery. I think it's beautiful how you care for your relatives and friends. I'm proud to be the wife of such a man."

Yet she would also need to make it clear how painful it was for her to be bumped for others so often: "Our date nights are so precious to me. It's so painful for me when you cancel. Then I start getting angry and feeling jealous of your relatives and friends. But I don't want you to stop being the loyal, giving person you are. I just need my time with you too. I miss you, Darnell."

Identifying and Expressing Fears

Are you having second thoughts about confronting your partner? Does the idea of sharing your complaints with him make you feel guilty or anxious?

Such feelings are normal. After all, confronting someone is risky. You could be ignored, criticized, or not taken seriously. You may be asking your partner for a closer relationship. Yet complaining about not being closer could end up pushing him away.

Perhaps you're conflicted about confronting your partner. On the one hand, you're hurting and need to speak up. On the other hand, you don't want to hurt your partner, especially since life has already hurt him and he's still suffering because of his trauma. In fact, you may be more aware of your partner's pain than he is.

It's important to recognize any anxieties and conflicting feelings you have about confronting your partner. If you wish, you can share some of these with your partner when you meet with him.

EXERCISE 4.6: My Fears and Feelings About Confronting My Partner

On a separate page in your journal, entitled "My Fears and Feelings About Confronting My Partner," answer the following questions.

1. How do you feel about talking to your partner about your grievances and asking for changes in your relationship? Write a few sentences about these feelings.

2. Do you have any mixed feelings about approaching him? Write a few sentences about any conflicting emotions you might be experiencing.

3. Would mentioning any of these feelings and concerns to your partner make you feel more comfortable? If so, which ones? Is it possible that bringing these up could also have a softening effect on your partner and make him more open to hearing what you have to say? If so, which feelings and concerns might you want to mention?

4. Write out how you would express the feelings and concerns you identified in number 3 to your partner. Here are some of the concerns Nina planned to share with Darnell: "I have to talk to you about something that's hard to talk about," "I need to tell you something, but I'm afraid it might push you away," and "I've spent a lot of time thinking about how to tell you about this problem, but I'm still not sure it's going to come out right."

    She also decided to say, "I feel guilty talking to you about this problem when you're so overwhelmed by work and other things. Because I care about you, I've put off talking to you about it for months. The last thing in the world I wanted to do was pressure someone who is already under so much pressure! But I couldn't wait any longer. If I didn't talk to you, I thought I'd burst."

Finalizing Your Message

You've already written out parts of your message in the above exercises. Now you're ready to pull together all these pieces and finalize what you're going to say to your partner.

Perhaps writing and rewriting your message so many times seems like overkill. But each time you write it out, you'll gain more insight into what's bothering you. You may also come up with more and better solutions and identify more positives. You may then need to revise your message.

EXERCISE 4.7: My Message to My Partner

On a separate page in your journal, entitled "My Message to My Partner," write out everything you plan to say to your partner using the communication skills in chapter 3 and the guidelines in this chapter. Include the following: one or two of the most important events that caused your grievance, your resulting feelings, your possible contributions to the problem, any anxieties or mixed feelings you have about confronting him that you feel you need to share or that might be helpful to share, some possible solutions to the problem, and as many positives as possible.

Don't make up positive things just to make him feel better or to try to manipulate him. Whatever positive comments you make need to be sincere.

When you present possible solutions, acknowledge the hardships they may impose on your partner. Also point out their possible benefits to him, what you're willing to do to help, and which solutions you like best.

Practicing Your Message

After you've written everything out, practice your message aloud. Keep rehearsing it until you feel comfortable with it. You can also practice with a therapist or trusted friend and ask for suggestions.

The more you practice, the more confident and relaxed you will feel during your discussion. However, you don't know what emotions might come up when you speak with your partner. You might be calmer than you thought you'd be. Or you might be more anxious, angry, or emotional than you expected. Either way, all the advance work you've done will help you remember your main points and express them more effectively. Since you've already released some of your anger beforehand and uncovered the positives, you're also more likely to have the right attitude.

Presenting Your Concerns

Now that you've completed your homework, you're ready to set up a time to present your partner with your complaint and suggested solutions. Follow the guidelines in "Getting Ready for Your Discussion," provided earlier in this chapter. Also consider the suggestions that follow.

Giving Your Partner Fair Warning

When you set up your meeting, be sure to mention the topic. Given your partner's history, he'll probably respond better to your complaints if he knows they're coming. Delivering negative feedback out of the blue to someone whose life was thrown off course by out-of-the-blue negative events is not recommended! The best way to tell your partner about your grievances is to present them during a meeting in which he's agreed to hear about them.

Helping Your Partner Feel Safe

Assure your partner that you'll be talking about only one issue, that you don't plan to criticize or blow up at him, and that he can call for a time-out any time he wants. Emphasize that you don't want to argue about who's right or wrong, because what you're talking about isn't a matter of right or wrong. It's a matter of emotion.

Make it clear that you're not asking him to discuss your issue right then and there. But if he wants to, that's fine. You'd also welcome any ideas he has about solving the problem.

For now, however, all you want is for him to hear you out. He's under no pressure to agree or disagree with any of your ideas for change right away. He can take some time to think about your message and get back to you later. But you hope that he does take the time to think about it because it's important to you.

If you want a response by a certain date, say so. If you're unsure what you'll do if he doesn't get back to you, say that if you don't hear from by that date, you may need to bring up the subject again.

When Your Partner Disregards Ground Rules or Other Agreements

If your partner disregards ground rules or other agreements, relationship expert Guerney (1987) offers the following suggestions.

1. Don't scold or criticize your partner. Instead tell him that this isn't what you remember agreeing to, and then repeat the agreement (for example, "We agreed not to name-call."). If you feel insulted, you don't have to explain why. Simply say, "That's not respectful" or "That's not appropriate."

2. If he's broken several ground rules, begin by mentioning only one. Offer to help him with it. Show him what to do. If he called you a name, for example, you could ask him what he was actually trying to say, or what feeling he was wanting to communicate.

3. If he won't accept your offer of help, repeat your offer.

4. If he still won't cooperate, you can either keep talking to him or tell him that you need to stop until he's willing to go along with your prior agreements.

When Communication Is Difficult or Impossible

What if there's a time-sensitive matter at hand and your partner won't communicate or makes communication impossible?

If you can handle the situation without his cooperation, you have two choices: The first is to let the matter ride, accept the consequences, and do what you can to prepare for them. The second is to decide on a solution without him, then tell him what action you plan to take, or what action you've already taken.

If you can't settle the matter by yourself, point out what could happen if he doesn't talk to you about it and the matter is left in limbo. Suggest going to a professional counselor, a member of the clergy, or a trusted friend or relative for help. If he won't go, consider going without him. Get help for both the immediate problem and the deeper issue of his inability or reluctance to communicate. Turn to family members, friends, and outside organizations for help as well.

In this chapter, you've learned how to prepare for and manage discussions about difficult subjects. You've also learned about the extra precautions and efforts involved in discussing relationship conflicts and complaints. You can find additional suggestions in the recommended self-help books on assertiveness and couples communication listed in the "Helpful Resources" section at the end of this book. You may need to modify those suggestions, however, in order to take into account your partner's PTSD and your unique personalities and circumstances.

The communication and discussion skills described in this chapter and in chapter 3 will be especially helpful when your partner is triggered into the PTSD cycle. In the next chapter, you'll learn ways of helping your partner—and yourself—during these stressful episodes.

CHAPTER 5

Managing Triggers and Trigger Reactions

If you want to kiss away my tears
Do not speak of my past
Speak only of love

—Greek folk song

A trigger is any person, place, thing, or situation associated with the trauma that sets off a PTSD symptom. Nina thought that therapy would stop Darnell from having PTSD "attacks" when he was triggered by reminders of his trauma. Darnell had hoped so too. He was tired of having nightmares every year on the Fourth of July. Sometimes he would sweat so much that the sheets had to be changed twice during the night.

Ten years of therapy later, Darnell is still having nightmares and Nina and Darnell are still doing extra laundry. "Why can't you be normal?" Nina can't help but wonder. Darnell wonders the same thing.

Like Nina and Darnell, you and your partner may want trigger reactions to disappear. Not only do they disrupt your lives, but they also keep the memories of the trauma alive, making the trauma seem never-ending.

It's important to understand that trigger reactions are forms of self-preservation. As described in chapter 1, they stem from fight-flight-freeze reactions that are hardwired into our bodies. However, therapy can show your partner constructive ways of managing his symptoms.

The hope is that increasing his control over his symptoms can help reduce their frequency and intensity. It can also lower the chance that his fears will turn into harmful obsessions or that his avoidance of certain situations will become a habit. In some cases, continued avoidance can lead to a condition called *agoraphobia*—extreme fear that can prevent a person from leaving home.

The negative impact of a trauma can be reduced by enjoying positive experiences that come one's way, thus creating a new history of positive experiences. Often these are referred to as restorative experiences. They can't erase the trauma, but they can lessen its importance. However, if a survivor's triggers prevent him from going certain places or doing certain things (or if the trauma shattered too much of his life), he may have difficulty building a new and more rewarding history that can counteract his traumatic experiences.

In this chapter you'll learn ways of helping your partner manage his triggers and improving the physical safety of your living environment. You'll also be provided with guidelines for talking to your partner about trauma, and for coping with two common triggers—medical appointments and social situations. Equally important, you'll work on finding ways of taking better care of yourself.

Hopefully your partner will work with you in completing the exercises and reviewing the suggestions in this chapter. However, if his triggers are likely to lead to panic attacks, suicide attempts, violence, binge drinking, or other destructive behavior, the suggestions in this section won't be enough. You'll also need to follow those provided in chapter 6.

The Nature of Triggers

Triggers are usually associated with the dangerous aspects of a trauma. But they can also be related to nondangerous parts. For example, a pedestrian injured by a speeding car may forever cringe at crosswalks. But if this incident occurred near a rose bush, he may be triggered by roses, or even all flowers.

Yet it could take him years to understand, or he may never understand, why he's so afraid of flowers. Either way, the fear can make him feel "crazier" than he already feels, and make others think he's "crazy" too.

Trigger Reactions

A minor reminder can cause a few hours of anxiety or a restless night's sleep. But a stronger trigger, or several small triggers occurring around the same time, can lead to a week of insomnia, panic attacks, fearfulness bordering on paranoia, or even suicidal thoughts. If your partner is already stressed by other problems, even a relatively small trigger can set off a severe reaction.

Unfortunately, sometimes survivors see their PTSD as punishment or payback for errors made in the past. When survivors (or those around them) believe that their PTSD is deserved, they can be less motivated to seek help.

Types of Triggers

Some triggers are time-limited, such as a specific date or a social event involving someone associated with the trauma. Other triggers—for example, a lawsuit—can last months or years. And still others are ongoing: a partner's eyes happen to be same exact shade of gray as those of someone who died in the trauma.

Some triggers are predictable, but others appear unexpectedly. Some are external; others, internal. External triggers come from other people, or the environment. Internal triggers come from within.

EXTERNAL TRIGGERS

Common external triggers include any sights, sounds, smells, touches, people, tasks, locations, dates, or situations associated with the trauma, especially those involving injustice, safety issues, or authority figures. Other common external triggers include discussions and media coverage about trauma; family and work pressures; negative local, national, or international events; life transitions; and physical confinement, such as jury duty, traffic jams, medical appointments, therapy sessions, or social events.

Anniversary reactions. Sometimes the connection between a particular date or season and a trauma is clear-cut. For instance, combat veterans may be triggered by the anniversary of being wounded or a buddy's death date. But they could also be triggered by the anniversary of their enlistment date. Similarly, a musician raped near a music store may be triggered not only by the anniversary of the assault, but also by the anniversary of when she started music lessons. Dates associated with suicide attempts, admission to psychiatric wards, or trauma-related medical procedures, or with the birth or death of one's abuser, can also be triggers.

INTERNAL TRIGGERS

Internal triggers can be any physical or emotional conditions similar to those experienced during the trauma.

Physical discomfort. Trauma usually involves some sort of physical stress. Consequently hunger, thirst, pain, illness, fatigue, sexual frustration, and other forms of physical discomfort can be triggers.

Strong emotions. Strong emotions can be triggers, especially feelings of loss or helplessness, or of being exploited, unprotected, trapped, or not in control of a situation.

Hence some survivors avoid funerals, hospitals, and even family members who are ill. Others avoid medical appointments because these appointments remind them of their mortality. Survivors may also dislike having to submit to the control of medical staff. This is especially the case if they had negative experiences with a helping professional or a health care institution. Survivors have even postponed treatment for cancer or other serious conditions for these reasons.

Sometimes aspects of a medical treatment resemble the trauma. For example, routine dental work can cause rape survivors to have flashbacks of oral rape. Dental drills can bring forth memories of other forms of sexual abuse.

Feelings toward partners. Unfortunately, survivors can be triggered by their feelings toward their partners. Loving someone means opening up oneself to that person. This is difficult for many people. But being emotionally open to others has terrible associations for survivors who were betrayed by people they trusted.

If your partner feels you haven't suffered as much as he has, he may resent you for seeming to have had an easier life than he has had. He may love you. But when he sees you being freer to laugh, cry, love, or have fun, he may also envy you. Perhaps the very qualities he cherishes in you remind him of how he was before his trauma or how he might have been if the trauma hadn't happened. For that reason, he may withdraw or start a quarrel with you at the very moment you're feeling at your best.

Although a part of him may feel inferior to you, another part may feel superior. Since you haven't been traumatized (or, in his view, he was traumatized more than you were), he may see you as being weaker, more naive, and untested by life. Yet having mixed feelings toward someone he loves may be confusing and overwhelming, and hence a trigger in itself.

Survivors of Multiple or Severe Traumas

For survivors of repeated or severe trauma, life is full of triggers. For them, ordinary details of life—such as breakfast, lunch, and dinner—can be triggers.

Amputees and others who bear physical scars due to their trauma can also be triggered on a daily basis. Abuse survivors who coped by cutting themselves or binge eating may have "battle scars," such as a misshapen body or razor marks on their legs. They can be triggered by those physical reminders every time they get dressed.

Trigger Reactions as Triggers

When PTSD symptoms are unexpected or overwhelming, they can be retraumatizing. For example, when Kitty is triggered, she feels as fearful, self-doubting, and angry as she did in the past. She may know that the situation triggering her isn't life-threatening. But because she can't stop herself from reacting as if the past was repeating itself, she feels as out of control as she did during her trauma.

Your partner may have mastered certain coping skills. Instead of taking days to manage a trigger reaction, now it takes only a few minutes. But those few minutes between his initial panic reaction and the time he begins using his coping skills can be frightening.

Categories of Triggers

Triggers can be divided into categories based on how difficult your partner feels they are to handle. He may view some as being relatively manageable right now, and others as possibly manageable in one year, or two. He may view others as being manageable only in the distant future—or maybe never. Over time, however, his view of a trigger's difficulty may change, especially with competent help.

Triggers can also be divided into categories based on their impact on your and your partner's lives:

1. **Category 1:** Triggers that may need to be avoided because they're emotionally or physically harmful

   Limiting contact with an abusive family member, for example, may be necessary because of the potential for being mistreated. But it isn't always easy to decide how advisable it may be to face a certain trigger. For example, going to court or filing a claim regarding a trauma-related issue could be emotionally and financially beneficial. Yet it can also be highly triggering. In addition, the course of the legal process and your partner's reactions to it are unpredictable. Hence the pros and cons of whether or not to proceed need to be carefully evaluated every step of the way.

2. **Category 2:** Triggers that can be wholly or partly avoided, at least temporarily, with few ill effects

   If your partner's trauma involved fire, for example, he may avoid barbecues because the smells remind him of burning flesh. Though he may want to attend a barbecue now and then, it's likely he can also choose to avoid them without any severe penalty.

3. **Category 3:** Triggers that create major emotional, financial, social, sexual, or other problems

129

Nina found it easy enough to go along with avoiding some of Darnell's category 2 triggers, such as certain movies and television programs. (She could always watch them on her own.) She also didn't mind trading chores with Darnell. It was his chore to take out the trash and hers to do the dishes. But since garbage bags reminded Darnell of body bags, they switched chores with no ill effects.

On the other hand, if Darnell were triggered by a coworker and wanted to quit his job, the consequences could have been staggering. Similarly, if your partner is triggered by driving, waiting, going to your child's graduation, or having sex in certain ways or at certain times, such triggers can create major problems. The same is true if he won't use needed doctors or visit important friends and relatives because they're located in neighborhoods associated with his trauma.

Supporting Your Partner's Efforts to Overcome His Triggers

Perhaps the main reason survivors seek help is to better handle the kinds of triggers in categories 2 and 3, especially those in category 3. The various kinds of trauma therapy described in chapter 7 can be beneficial.

One of these therapies, called exposure therapy, involves exposing survivors to their problem triggers in a gradual and safe manner. This gradual exposure can help survivors learn that their triggers aren't as dangerous as what happened during the trauma.

You can learn more about exposure and other trauma therapies in chapters 6 and 7 and from books on trauma recovery. (See the "Helpful Resources" section at the end of this book.) However, under no circumstances should you try to play the role of therapist and conduct some kind of exposure or other trauma therapy on your partner by yourself.

Some of these therapies may seem relatively simple and straight-forward. But they're actually quite complex. Unless they're conducted by a qualified PTSD specialist, they can easily backfire. Even thera-pists can misjudge a client's readiness to face a certain trigger, or can somehow pressure a client into facing a trigger prematurely. Or per-haps the client is the one who's in a hurry. The client can then relapse, and may end up unwilling to work on that trigger ever again.

You can be supportive by meeting with your partner and his ther-apist to discuss the approach and methods being used and ask what you can do to help. But don't be dismayed if, at first and perhaps for quite some time, your partner can take only baby steps toward coping with a particular trigger.

Suppose he's triggered by crowds, but wants to attend your son's games. In therapy it's decided that he could begin by attending games for a half hour and then leaving. A part of you may be overjoyed that he's making some kind of effort to be there. Yet another part of you may feel he's being ridiculous.

There's nothing that scary about school athletic events, you may think. Shouldn't he just force himself to go a few times and stay? Isn't that the only way he'll learn that his fears are illogical and that he's only been hurting himself and the family by staying away?

You may feel like saying something like, "Only a half-hour? Can't you stay at least an hour? Come on, you can do it! It's not that hard. Your friend Jim went through the same kind of "trauma," and he can go to his son's games with no problem."

Perhaps you'd like your partner to stay the entire time because you want to share the experience with him, or you know how important it is for your son. You may also be tired of being the one who always has to take your child to games. Or perhaps you simply want to help free your partner from what you feel are unnecessary chains.

But if you try to encourage him as described above, he may or may not feel encouraged. Most likely he'll feel humiliated and pressured. He's probably just as aware as you are that going to games is quite safe. Yet his body begins to panic (or shut down) at the very thought of going. Knowing that he's disappointing you and the family creates even more stress and only increases his panic (or numbing).

A more supportive response would be, "That's great! I know how hard these games can be for you. That you're willing to come anyway shows how much you care about us. Of course I'd love it if you could stay longer, but I'm just happy you're coming. Whatever I can do to make it more enjoyable, let me know."

Your warm, accepting attitude creates an island of emotional safety for him in the midst of a situation that the traumatized part of him feels is dangerous. This sense of safety increases the chances of his coming to the next game, and then, perhaps, the one after that. Over time, he may be able to stay longer and longer because he's slowly learning it's safe.

Like any other form of therapy, exposure therapy doesn't work for everyone. But in one case, with the help of exposure and other kinds of therapy, a survivor who was afraid to set foot in a PTA meeting eventually became the PTA president. If his wife had openly scorned his first, limited attempts to attend the meetings, she'd have given him yet another reason to stay away. Instead, she helped make the experience safer and more pleasant by not challenging his limits and by keeping her judgmental thoughts to herself.

Coping with Long-Standing Triggers

It's far more difficult for partners of survivors to be patient with category 3 triggers. Unfortunately, some of these triggers can be long-lasting, because they're associated with severe trauma or with an ongoing or recurring negative situation related to the trauma. Hence your partner may try hard and long to manage a certain trigger, but make little progress.

For example, Darnell enjoyed traveling prior to and during his tour of duty. But today he's triggered by almost any form of travel. In part, this is because of his experiences with car bombs and with being tortured in a truck. In addition, upon his return, his first wife claimed he was an unfit father due to his PTSD. In the dozens of court-related appointments and hearings that followed, Darnell's personality and PTSD were often mocked. Each one of his court appearances involved a two-hour commute. After he lost many of his parental rights in court, Darnell never wanted to set foot in a car again.

He could drive to work and run local errands. But he couldn't take day trips to the country or fly anywhere without paying a huge price in anxiety and other symptoms.

For ten years Darnell tried various kinds of therapy. Eventually his psychiatrist concluded that the amount of distress Darnell experienced during travel was directly proportional to the amount of physical confinement involved. That meant that if Darnell were stuck in a vehicle or an airport for four hours instead of two, he'd become twice as triggered. It would also take him twice as long to regain his emotional and physical balance. Hence the doctor advised Darnell to limit travel.

This long-lasting trigger prevented Darnell from accepting a promotion because it involved frequent travel. Nina (Darnell's second wife) had dreamed of going on cruises with Darnell. She at least wanted to go the beach once in a while. She was very disappointed that Darnell simply couldn't do these things without being miserable.

Accepting Darnell's travel problem wasn't easy. At first Nina was angry and kept suggesting ways of making travel more pleasant. But eventually she realized she had two choices: she could exhaust herself arguing and pressuring Darnell, or she could simply accept the reality and grieve the losses that came with it.

But she didn't come to this realization overnight or because someone told her to simply "let go" and "live and let live." It took many years, many tears, and many discussions with others before Nina could accept Darnell's limitations.

She then began taking responsibility for fulfilling some of her travel dreams on her own. But there were still times she felt sad or angry about Darnell's inability to join her.

It helped Nina to realize that Darnell had to go through the painful process of accepting the serious limitations caused by his long-lasting trigger, just like she did. It also helped her to view this trigger as a battle injury, rather than as a sign that Darnell had somehow failed therapy, or that she had failed him. "If Darnell were wounded in battle or had a medical problem that made traveling difficult, everyone would understand," she told herself. Nobody would be mad at him, including me. But this travel problem is just as much a battle wound as a physical injury that can be seen. It has biological roots, too—and it's hard to fight biology, especially the biology of being in a war and then being deprived of your children because of it.

"So what if we don't have more money or don't go on trips? Darnell could have died overseas! At least I still have him, and we still love each other. And the fact that he has limits helps him accept mine."

Indeed, in my clinical experience, survivors who are aware of the problems caused by their long-standing triggers are less likely to demand that their partners be without flaws or problems of their own. Furthermore, nothing is forever. As your partner becomes better able to manage his other triggers, or if his life circumstances should improve, he may be able to make headway on a trigger that seems permanent.

Remember also that every relationship has its issues, and all people have certain limitations. You may be disappointed that your mate can't participate in certain activities you enjoy. But there are probably many nontraumatized people who don't or can't enjoy those activities, either.

If a certain activity is important to you, then you may need to pursue it—with or without your partner. He, in turn, will need to set aside any jealousy he may feel and not stand in your way.

Creating a Physically Safe Living Environment

You can reduce the impact of your partner's triggers—and help yourself as well—by improving the safety of your living environment. Since triggers create fear, the safer she feels at home and in her environment, the better.

Listed below are some ideas for creating a sense of physical safety. Although beneficial, these actions involve certain emotional, financial, and other costs. Only you and your partner can decide if a particular suggestion's benefits outweigh its costs.

HOME SAFETY

1. Have adequate locks on windows and doors. Keep them locked at appropriate times. Check fire extinguishers, smoke alarms, and carbon-monoxide detectors regularly.

2. Take care of any electrical problems, faulty gas appliances, and structural problems, such as unstable stairs or leaky roofs.

3. If crime is a concern, consider getting an alarm system or a dog, starting or joining a neighborhood-watch group, or getting to know your neighbors better. If you live (or work) in a particularly dangerous area, consider relocating (or finding work) somewhere safer.

4. Prepare for power outages, natural disasters, and other emergencies. Follow the guidelines provided by your power providers, county and state government, and the Department of

Homeland Security. You can obtain this information directly from these organizations, a library, or the Internet.

5. Make copies of all important papers (birth certificates, credit cards, and so forth) and put the originals in a safe-deposit box.

6. Review your insurance policies to make sure you have adequate coverage.

7. Secure any weapons or hazardous materials.

8. Avoid contact with people with tendencies toward or histories of violence, or whose lifestyles involve crime or contact with criminals.

9. Eliminate dangerous habits, such as smoking in bed. If a family member won't take necessary precautions, seek help immediately.

VEHICULAR SAFETY

1. Make sure cars, motorcycles, bicycles, and other vehicles are safe and have adequate insurance coverage.

2. Use seat belts, helmets, and other safety features faithfully.

WORK AND SCHOOL SAFETY

1. Review the safety codes in your and your partner's workplaces and your children's schools. See if these codes are adequate and are being enforced. If not, consider whether you and your partner have the time and other resources to contact the proper authorities or to participate in some type of formal action to correct these violations.

2. If your or your partner's employers or your children's school can't or won't make necessary safety improvements, think about what you can do to make yourselves safer. Would it be helpful to take certain precautions or teach your children certain skills?

3. Make sure you and your family are protected from any weapons or hazardous materials in your work environment or on school property.

HEALTH ISSUES

1. Make sure you, your partner, and others in your household have regular physical and dental checkups, and don't miss medical appointments.

2. If you have health insurance, see if it is adequate. If it's inadequate, or if you don't have insurance, contact your state medical, dental, and mental health associations and local hospitals and clinics to inquire about low-cost or free services.

3. If your partner resists medical care, consider the suggestions in the section titled "Encouraging Your Partner to Seek Help," in chapter 7. Even if she won't go, you can. She'll feel safer knowing that you and other family members are taking care of your health.

4. Have a list of phone numbers and contact information for emergency medical and mental health assistance. Keep a copy handy and on your person.

5. Consider whether an exercise or self-defense class might make you or your partner feel safer and stronger.

Identifying Triggers

In addition to improving physical safety, there are other ways you can help your partner manage her triggers. The first step is to identify the triggers and their effects.

EXERCISE 5.1: My Partner's Triggers

Review the list of common internal and external triggers provided earlier in this chapter. Then, on a separate page in your journal, entitled "My Partner's Triggers," answer the following questions:

1. Which people, places, things, touches, tasks, dates, emotions, physical conditions, or situations seem to increase your partner's PTSD? List as many triggers as you wish.

    Keep in mind that anniversary reactions don't necessarily occur on the exact date of the anniversary. They can start a few days to a week before or after. For example, Darnell's depression starts the week before the Fourth of July. Once the fireworks are over, so are his nightmares—until the next trigger. In contrast, Kitty's nightmares start the day after her father's birthday.

2. Do any vehicular or other accidents, illnesses, or flare-ups your partner has had (with you or with others) seem to occur fairly regularly around a particular date, or during or after certain types of situations? Might these dates and situations be triggers? If so, add these to your list.

3. Is she triggered by change, such as at work or in the family? Include these on your list.

4. If possible, review your list with your partner. Make it crystal clear that you aren't asking her to explain why these particular people and situations trigger her, nor are you asking her

for details about her trauma. You simply want to know if your list is accurate. Perhaps she can add to the list.

While creating and reviewing your list, consider reading about trauma or talking with other survivors or a trained mental health professional. (See the "Helpful Resources" section.)

5. If you wish, put on your calendar any triggers having to do with specific dates.

Identifying Your Partner's Trigger Reactions and Their Impact on You

You can better prepare for your partner's trigger times if you're aware of her trigger reactions and how they affect you. If she reacts the exact same way to every trigger, then you needn't complete the following exercise. More likely, however, her reactions differ in kind and in degree from one trigger to the next. Your responses to her reactions may also vary.

EXERCISE 5.2: My Partner's Trigger Reactions

On a separate page in your journal, entitled "My Partner's Trigger Reactions," write a few sentences about how your partner tends to react to each specific trigger you listed in exercise 5.1. Which particular symptoms does this trigger tend to bring forth? Does she become more anxious or more shut down—or does she cycle between the two?

Include her reactions to you and others during these times. Some triggers may make her more sexual or more demanding of your attention. Others may have the opposite effect. Or perhaps there's no pattern. What happens in your home?

EXERCISE 5.3: How My Partner's Trigger Reactions Affect Me

Review your entries for exercise 5.2. Then, on a separate page in your journal, entitled "How My Partner's Trigger Reactions Affect Me," describe how your partner's reactions to each specific trigger affect your schedule, health, mood, self-esteem, and relationships with others. How do they affect others who care about her?

Preparing for Triggers

In this section, you'll learn various ways of preparing for and coping with your partner's triggers. You'll also work on identifying your needs and developing a self-care plan.

Learning from the Past

Couples often throw up their hands and say, "We don't know what to do! We don't have any coping skills!" But they do have some coping skills. They just aren't aware of them.

As long as you and your partner are still together and still trying to take care of the basics of life, then you're obviously doing something right.

EXERCISE 5.4: Learning from the Past: Safe and Helpful Approaches to Trigger Reactions

In this exercise you'll write about how you and your partner have coped with triggers in the past. You'll then identify which approaches have been helpful and which have not. In this exercise and all that follow, only those ideas that are safe can be considered helpful. Violence, substance abuse, self-cutting, overspending, and other destructive behaviors are not safe.

On a separate page in your journal, entitled "Learning from the Past: Safe and Helpful Approaches to Trigger Reactions," follow these instructions:

1. Review your journal entries for exercise 5.1. Looking back, list all the safe ways your partner tried to manage her trigger reactions that were helpful. Include any safe action she took that seemed to help, if only sometimes or a small amount. Don't limit yourself to psychological techniques. Did having a glass of juice, sitting in her favorite room, or saying a short prayer bring her any relief?

2. List unhelpful or unsafe way she tried to cope.

3. List safe ways that you tried to assist her that helped, even if only a little.

4. List anything you said or did that didn't help or was unsafe.

If possible, share your entries with your partner and ask for feedback.

Identifying Your Needs

When your partner's triggered, her needs are pressing. It's still important, however, to try to take care of yourself. Notice the word *try*. During some of her most severe trigger times, you may need to set aside some of your needs.

Other times, however, within the limits of the situation, self-care should be a major priority. Your needs deserve special consideration because your well-being is essential to both you and your partner. But first you need to have a clear picture of what your needs are.

Self-Care: The Basics

Self-care begins with the body: having proper nutrition and adequate rest and exercise, and taking care of your medical needs. But your emotional, social, and mental needs matter too. Emotionally, you may need time for yourself, as well as for others. Mentally, you may need to keep your life interesting by learning new things or developing certain interests. This may involve pursuing friendships and activities both with your partner and separately.

Financially, you need to be able to meet your current needs and prepare for emergencies. You may also have spiritual and creative needs.

If you weren't in a relationship, you'd be able to meet your needs more fully and freely. Partnership can make it more difficult. Yet even in the midst of your many commitments, a basic minimum of your various needs must be met. No matter how much you love your partner, you can't make her (or others) your entire life. If you don't take care of yourself, eventually you'll be drained and have little left to give.

EXERCISE 5.5: My Basic Needs

In this exercise you'll define what self-care means for you in the different categories described above. On a separate page in your journal, entitled "My Basic Needs," answer the following questions:

1. What are your nutritional needs? What do you need to eat and when?

2. How much sleep and exercise do you need to stay healthy? Ideally? At a bare minimum?

3. What medical needs must you tend to?

4. What helps you deal with your feelings? How often do you need to do these things to keep your spirits up and help stay emotionally balanced?

5. How much time do you need for yourself apart from others? With your partner? With others? For each of these, how much time do you feel is absolutely necessary?

6. What mental, creative, or spiritual activities make your life more interesting and fulfilling and make you feel more alive? How often do you need to be involved in these activities to avoid becoming bored or depressed?

7. What are your financial goals and limits? What do you need to do to feel safer financially?

EXERCISE 5.6: My Self-Care Plan

In this exercise you'll develop a self-care plan. Depending on what happens during a particular trigger episode, you may or may not be able to use all, or even part, of your plan. But it's important to have one.

On a separate page in your journal, entitled "My Self-Care Plan," follow these instructions:

1. Review your journal entries for exercise 5.2. Reflecting back on these experiences, what did you need to do for yourself? List these needs. Include any that you felt you had to set aside because of your partner's condition. Also include any of the basic needs you described in exercise 5.5.

2. Have you ever tried to meet the needs you listed in number 1 when your partner was triggered? Be specific.

3. Which self-care efforts proved difficult or unsafe? Which ones were both successful and safe?

4. Looking back, is there anything more you might have done to safely reduce your stress? If it wasn't possible to meet a particular need in full, could it have been met in part? If taking a long, hot bath wasn't possible, would a quick shower have helped? If you had to cancel a meeting with a friend, would a brief phone conversation have been possible? (See "Developing a Support System" in chapter 7 and the "Helpful Resources" section for a list of books on stress management and self-care.)

5. Review your replies to numbers 1 through 5. Then list all the ways you could possibly have taken care of yourself, even in part, when your partner was triggered. Also note any preparations you need to make so you'll be able to act on your self-care ideas in the future.

    Who do you need to call? What food or other supplies (such as your favorite DVDs or art supplies) do you need to have on hand?

    Having this list doesn't mean that you'll be able to find a way to meet both your partner's needs and your own during her trigger times. If you expect this, you'll only end up feeling like a failure. But you may be able to act on parts of this list, circumstances permitting.

6. When your partner is distressed and unavailable to you, how can you safely cope with any feelings of rejection, abandonment, or loneliness you might be experiencing?

    You'll still hurt. But there are ways of giving yourself some comfort. To whom could you turn for emotional support? Would writing down your feelings help? What activities would be comforting or fulfilling to you? List these people and activities.

7. Are you angry because your partner has cut herself off from you emotionally or sexually because of her trigger reaction?

Are you feeling controlled by her triggers and the stresses they create?

Telling her how angry you are with her (or with her PTSD) when she's triggered may not be productive. Until she's more approachable, consider releasing your frustrations by talking to supportive others, journaling, or writing a letter to her, as you did in exercise 4.1, in chapter 4. (Follow the instructions provided and do not share your letter with your partner.)

You could also channel your anger energy into activities such as exercise, gardening, or working on project.

(See the "Helpful Resources" section for a list of books on coping with anger, loneliness, and other difficult emotions.)

Talking to Your Partner About Triggers

If your partner is willing, discuss working together as a team to help manage her triggers. If she's in therapy or a recovery program, perhaps she's received specific suggestions about handling triggers. If she'll share them with you, write them down.

Share your observations about what she did in the past that seemed to help or not help, based on your replies to exercise 5.4. Ask her opinion about anything you learned from reading about trauma recovery, talking with other survivors, or meeting with her therapist.

Don't present these ideas as surefire solutions, because they're not. Some ideas work for some people but not others, or work sometimes but not every time. Nevertheless, it can't hurt for her to be aware of available methods, especially if she's not getting help.

Ask how you and others might help. What would she like for you to do when she's having a nightmare or flashback, or spacing out?

Don't go along with unhealthy suggestions, such as supplying her with alcohol or drugs.

Mention anything safe you did in the past that seemed to help, based on your replies to exercise 5.4. If she has specific safe ideas about how you can help, write them down. Tell her you'll try to remember them. But if you forget, you want her to remind you.

Be clear about what you can and can't do to help. If you're not willing or able to help in all the ways she wants, are there any safe parts of her request that you could handle comfortably? Brainstorm with her about ways of getting her other needs met safely.

Share relevant aspects of your self-care plan with her. Emphasize that whatever you might do for yourself isn't a rejection of her. For example, if she wants to be alone, you may go do something else. But you'll try to be available if she changes her mind and wants your company.

Additional Suggestions

Before an expected trigger (or during a prolonged one), consider the following suggestions:

1. Stick to your usual routine as much as possible. Make nonessential activities optional. Avoid additional commitments or make them tentative.

2. Avoid exposure to trauma in the media and elsewhere. Minimize contact with as many other stressors as possible.

3. Use available sources of emotional support. Consider extra therapy appointments or 12-step meetings. Inquire about contacting therapists or sponsors by phone on an as-needed basis.

4. Within reason, be available to your partner for holding, talking, or doing something relaxing together. (See the guidelines listed under "Talking About Trauma," later in this chapter.)

5. Make extra efforts to take good care of yourselves physically, including proper nutrition, exercise, rest, and taking prescribed medications as directed. Have all necessary medications on hand.

6. Have a copy of your self-care plan handy.

7. Have an updated list of contact information for emergency medical and mental health services (including hotline numbers for suicide crises and family violence) and for other supports (for both you and your partner), such as friends, relatives, spiritual advisors, or any 12-step program sponsors.

8. Consider healthy forms of distraction, such as short walks and other safe, nontriggering forms of entertainment. Have on hand DVDs, music, museum schedules, and so on.

Commemorating the Trauma

Sometimes survivors are helped by doing something with others that says, "This is what happened to me. It was terrible. It hurt then, and it hurts now."

Here are some ideas: create a ritual or attend a formal religious service; plant a tree or beautify nature in some way; listen to music or read poems on the theme of trauma; visit a public monument that has special meaning to your partner; make a charitable donation; help someone in need; light a candle and have a moment of silence together.

Coping with Medical and Dental Appointments

The following suggestions can help reduce the stress of medical and dental appointments:

1. Avoid scheduling routine appointments close to anniversary dates. When possible, space out appointments.

2. Schedule routine appointments well in advance so they can be at convenient times.

3. If waiting makes your partner anxious, ask for the first appointment in the morning or after lunch. Contact the medical office an hour or two before the appointment to see if the doctor is on schedule.

4. Would it be helpful to bring along something to do (a book or music) or something to eat while waiting? Or to have someone go with your partner, or talk to her about her appointment before or after?

5. Write down questions for the medical staff in advance. Have your partner bring contact information for people to call in case she needs support or a ride home.

6. Find out the length and nature of the appointment, what procedures might be done and why, what instruments will be used, whether physical pain might be involved, who will be in the room, and what options are available. Learn more about these options by talking to others or getting information from the Internet or a library.

7. Suggest to your partner that she take notes on the medical staff's answers to her questions.

8. Remind her that she doesn't have to agree to any procedure on the spot. Unless the matter is urgent, she can take time to think about her options and get second and third opinions.

9. If a particular physician or clinic isn't supportive, consider finding a new one.

Coping with Social Situations

Triggers may prevent your partner from attending social and family functions. Perhaps being in the same room or area for a certain period of time makes her feel trapped. Or perhaps she's triggered by certain aspects of the physical setting or the activities. For example, if her first marriage was abusive, she may dislike going to weddings.

You may, therefore, have to choose between attending an event alone and missing out on it. Another option is to structure events so they are less triggering. Some events will remain off-limits for her—at least for now. But you can probably increase the number of events you can attend together by following the suggestions provided below. The key concepts in these suggestions are control, creativity, and compromise.

1. Find out everything you can about the event: the location, travel time, duration, any scheduled activities, who and how many people will be there, and so forth. All details are important.

2. Discuss your and your partner's reasons for attending or not attending. What parts of the event would be most and least enjoyable to you? To your partner?

3. Identify the specific triggers involved in the event.

4. Is it possible to attend the agreeable parts of the event and avoid the most disagreeable or most triggering parts? If there's little overlap between the parts you and your partner wish to attend, try to compromise. (Some situations lend themselves to compromise. Others don't.)

5. Discuss ways of reducing the triggers involved for your partner. Ask, "What would make it possible for you to go?" Ask the same question with respect to yourself.

6. Establish a safety plan. If the situation becomes increasingly difficult for your partner, have a prearranged way of communicating that. Decide on a code word, gesture, or other nonverbal signal that says, "It's time to go." (See chapters 3 and 4 for suggestions.) Be sure that whatever way you decide to communicate doesn't draw the attention of others.

7. Establish alternative exit plans. The more sure your partner feels that she will be able to comfortably leave a situation, the easier it will be for her to enter that situation. The same holds true for you.

   Discuss ways of leaving that won't embarrass you or your partner, or upset your hosts or other guests. You needn't lie or make elaborate excuses. You can simply say, "We need to be going home now."

8. Set the stage for your exit plans. For example, if your partner feels she can tolerate only part of an event, tell your hosts in advance that you'll be coming late or leaving early.

9. If you want to attend more, or a different part, of the event than your partner does, try to arrange the necessary transportation.

10. After attending an event, discuss what could've been done to make it more manageable and pleasurable for both of you.

Remember that the more freedom of choice you can give each other, the easier it will be to figure out ways of making an event more manageable and rewarding.

Getting Through Trigger Reactions

Here are some suggestions for getting through trigger reactions:

1. Go to a safe place, preferably one with a toilet nearby, in case your partner begins having symptoms like nausea or diarrhea.

2. If your partner's having a flashback, a nightmare, or night terrors, ground her in present-day reality by telling her where she is—including the address, the date, and your name—and assuring her that she's safe. You could also remind her of upcoming plans, have her touch or focus her eyes on a safe item (such as a chair or a piece of cloth), say her name (or your name) aloud several times, or describe the room she's in or the weather outside.

3. During a flashback or a nightmare, don't come up behind your partner without announcing your presence. Don't touch her without asking first. Otherwise she might feel she's being attacked.

4. Ask what you can do to help. Even if you've already discussed this, ask again. Each episode of being triggered is unique. What she thought would be helpful when you made plans may not be what she needs at the moment. If she suggests something different from what she suggested in the past, don't point this out to her—unless her suggestion is unsafe.

5. If she's at a loss as to how you can help her or how she can help herself, offer to remind her of some of the ideas you discussed when you were planning for this trigger—such as suggestions given to her by a therapist, 12-step sponsor, or other advisor—and of things that helped her in the past (listed in number 1 and number 3 in exercise 5.4). Offer to sit quietly with her as long as she would like. Suggest that she call her therapist or 12-step sponsor.

6. If she's open to listening to you, you could offer comfort and support by making one or more of these statements:

   a. Right now you're remembering the trauma (or feeling as you did during the trauma). But that doesn't mean that the trauma is happening again (or that it will happen soon).

   b. Being triggered is normal. It doesn't mean you're inadequate. It means your survival instinct and your central nervous system are in good working order.

   c. Anyone who thinks you're wallowing in the past or feeling sorry for yourself doesn't know a thing about PTSD!

   d. What's troubling you is serious and might feel like a matter of life or death. But nobody's going to die.

   e. If you're grieving something that happened in the past, that means you have feelings. If you're feeling guilty about something, that means you have a sense of right and wrong.

   f. You can get through this. I'm here for you. Others care about you too.

   g. Maybe you don't feel so strong right now. But it takes a very strong person to go through all these triggers and not hurt herself or others. Think how much better the world would be if everyone had as much self-control and ability to tolerate emotional pain as you do.

7. If she says she doesn't want to hear your suggestions or comforting words, or if they seem to be making her upset or distant, stop talking.

8. If she wants you stay with her, try to do so. Let her know, however, that if at some point she feels she needs some space, you won't be offended and could busy yourself with another activity nearby.

9. If she wants to be left alone, tell her where you'll be and how to reach you if she changes her mind.

10. Make her as physically comfortable as possible. Have food and water available. Adjust the temperature, if necessary. Being thirsty or hungry, or too hot or too cold, can intensify trigger reactions and can be triggers in themselves. Don't let yourself become dehydrated or hungry, either.

11. Take care of yourself as best you can. Refer to the self-care plan you developed in exercise 5.6 for ideas.

12. Don't make major decisions during a trigger reaction.

13. Depending on how anxious or numb your partner is, it may not be advisable for her to drive; cook; stand on ladders; take care of children; handle fragile items, chemicals, weapons, scissors, saws, or other potentially dangerous items; or participate in sports that require focus, balance, or concentrated effort. If you aren't sure what to do, call a trained mental health professional, your family physician, or a mental health hotline.

14. Be alert for signs of severe reactions requiring your immediate action or medical attention. (See chapter 6.)

Talking About Trauma

During your partner's trigger times, she may need distance from you. Yet these could be the very times she wants to talk about her trauma.

Let Your Partner Set the Pace

Let her know you're willing to listen. But never pressure her to share. Assure her that if she's in the middle of sharing something and wants to stop, that's fine with you. You're glad to listen, but she needn't push herself to finish her story for your sake. She can always finish another time, when and if she feels like it.

While listening, don't ask questions like a detective, or ask for detailed descriptions of her worst moments or a particularly gory scene. If she was sexually assaulted, don't ask for sexual details. If she never tells you what happened, that doesn't mean she doesn't love or trust you. She may not remember what happened, or she may be trying to forget.

The Power of Presence

Perhaps you feel you aren't being empathic enough, or you don't know what to say. But there's value in just being present in a loving way. What she may really need is not the right words or solutions to her agony, but someone who can assure her she'll make it through, or someone who will listen without making critical comments.

Judging Your Partner

Yet as you listen to your partner's story, you may find yourself judging her. Despite your compassion, you may also wonder why she didn't act more courageously, wisely, or ethically during her trauma. A part of you may even think that if her trauma had happened to you, you would've reacted better than she did. You may then feel guilty, as if you are secretly betraying her.

Judgmental attitudes toward survivors are, however, widespread throughout our society. Even if you disagree with such attitudes, you can't help but be affected by them. They can also be a way of protecting yourself from your partner's pain.

Or they could indicate that you need to learn more about trauma. It's likely that the more you learn, the less judgmental you'll be. If your critical attitudes continue, there may be deeper issues in your relationship that need to be explored.

Earlier in this book you were advised to not keep secrets from your partner. But there's no need to share your critical thoughts with her. Talk about them with someone else.

Disbelieving Your Partner

As your partner tells her story, you may sometimes wonder if she's telling the truth. Perhaps you have trouble accepting that such terrible things could actually happen. Maybe the details of her story vary from one telling to the next, or she can't remember half of what she described the time before.

Traumatic memories are not stored the same way as other memories are. It's normal for periods of remembering to be followed by periods of forgetting. It's also normal for some memories to be vivid, while others are completely or partially repressed. Traumatic memories also vary over time in terms of content. But it is your partner's emotional reactions to her memories that need to be the focus of your attention, provided they don't cause you to become dysfunctional.

Setting Limits

Though you want to be supportive, there may be a limit to how much of your partner's pain and trauma you're willing or able to listen to. If she's just shared a particularly heartbreaking or terrifying episode with you, it would be normal to find yourself thinking about her and her trauma for a few hours, or even a day or two, afterward.

This is the same way you might feel after hearing about something terrible in the news, such as a gunman shooting people at a mall. Sometimes images and thoughts of these traumas linger in our hearts and minds for a while. Such thoughts and feelings are a normal part of being compassionate.

But if your reactions are more than temporary and begin to affect your ability to function, it may be time to back off. This doesn't mean you'll never listen again, but perhaps you can't listen as long as a trained professional. If you're also a survivor, then listening to your partner's trauma could retraumatize you in some ways. If it brings your PTSD to the surface, you may definitely need to set limits.

Even trained trauma therapists need to limit their caseload. If, out of compassion, they take on too many cases, they may begin having headaches, other body aches, or PTSD-like symptoms such as nightmares and depression. They may also develop a cynical or hostile attitude toward their clients as a way of distancing themselves from their clients' pain. If you listen past your limits, you may have similar reactions (Ortlepp and Friedman 2002).

You needn't be concerned about a single nightmare, or a day of two of feeling anxious about your safety or angry at the dark side of life. But if these or other PTSD-like symptoms persist, or if you develop any physical or other symptoms, you need to seek professional guidance before you continue listening to your partner. You may also need help with your symptoms.

When you set limits, assure your partner that you aren't rejecting her. You could say, for example, "I want to be there for you, but your trauma sometimes overwhelms me. If I'm so affected by just hearing about what happened to you, this shows me how awful it was for you, who actually went through it. It's given me a new respect for you as a survivor.

"I'm hoping that a counselor can help me find ways of listening that are manageable for me. But just as you need to limit certain activities because they are too triggering, I may need to do the same."

Keep in mind, also, that your ability or desire to listen to your partner's trauma may vary. Some days you may be feeling too stressed or emotionally vulnerable to listen. If that's the case, and you're the only one your partner has to talk to about her trauma, it may be time to encourage her to seek help. (See chapter 7 for suggestions.)

Establishing Greater Intimacy

Listening to your partner's trauma can be stressful. Yet it can bring you closer together, provided you don't develop long-term or severe symptoms due to listening. That she can open up to you is a sign of trust. She trusts that you will respect her wounds and not create new ones.

Honor that trust as best you can. But trauma is a highly sensitive subject. No matter how hard you try to respond caringly, someday you're bound to do or say something that offends her.

Prepare for this. Tell her in advance that if she's upset by one of your reactions, you want to know. You'd much rather she tell you up front than decide she'll never share her trauma with you again.

If you do accidentally wound her, simply apologize. Then do your best not to wound her in the same way again. Your partner's feelings have probably been trampled on many times by people who didn't care if they hurt her. So a sincere apology could go a long way. Hopefully she'll treat you as tenderly when she wounds you.

The next chapter provides suggestions for coping with panic attacks, rage reactions, domestic violence, addiction, and suicide crises.

CHAPTER 6

Crises: Panic Attacks, Rage Reactions, Domestic Violence, Addiction, and Suicide

The panic attacks, rage reactions, family violence, addiction, and suicidal wishes associated with PTSD can lead to major medical problems, injury, and death. These crises can also have serious consequences for partners.

This chapter provides ideas for doing your part to help avert these crises and for coping with them until outside help is available. These ideas are not meant to suggest that you can actually prevent such crises or manage them on your own. It bears repeating that this book's recommendations are no substitute for medical and mental health treatment.

Prepare for these crises by having a list of contact information for emergency mental health and medical services, as described in chapter 5. Keep it with you at all times. Ask your partner to do the same.

Panic Attacks

Panic attacks are experiences of extreme fear during which people feel as if they're dying, losing their minds, or having a heart attack. Some people freeze; others become hysterical. If your partner is crying, shaking, or sweating, his panic attack may be obvious. But if he's so frightened by his symptoms that he can barely move, his panic attack might not show. After the first panic attack, most people live in fear of having another one.

According to the *DSM-5* (APA 2013, 214), a panic attack is an "abrupt surge of intense fear or intense discomfort that reaches a peak within minutes." During the attack, four or more of the following symptoms occur:

1. Heart palpitations, rapid heart rate, or pounding heart

2. Sweating

3. Trembling or shaking

4. Feeling short of breath or smothered

5. Choking sensations

6. Pain or discomfort in the chest

7. Nausea or upset stomach

8. Dizziness or light-headedness

9. Hot flushes or chills

10. Tingling sensations or numbness

11. Feelings of unreality or detachment from oneself

12. Fear of insanity or losing control

13. Fear of dying

What Causes Panic Attacks?

Panic attacks are often brought on by stressful circumstances, such as a death in the family, a failed romance, or a work deadline. They're particularly common among people with untreated depression, PTSD, or another disorder (Burns 2007).

Symptoms associated with panic attacks can also arise from substance abuse, parasites, hypoglycemia, or inner-ear or heart problems. When medical conditions or substances cause the symptoms, it's not technically a panic attack. Yet sometimes symptoms result from both stress and medical problems. It's therefore important not to rule out physical contributions to your partner's panic attacks.

Helping Prevent Panic Attacks

Check to see if your partner's panic attack symptoms are a side effect of any of his medications. Encourage him to have a complete medical examination, avoid alcohol and caffeine, follow an approved exercise program, obtain medical advice before changing the doses of his medications, and be screened for depression.

IDENTIFYING PATTERNS

Any kind of advance warning can make a big difference. Do your partner's panic attacks tend to occur in certain locations or situations, or around certain people or dates? If there's a pattern, prepare for these attacks as you did for triggers in chapter 5.

Does your partner tend to complain about any particular physical problems right before his attacks, such as dizziness or feeling like he's losing control of his bowels? These could be signs of an upcoming attack. Knowing what he tends to think or feel before an attack could provide a five- or ten-minute warning. Even a three-minute warning can help reduce the shock aspect of a panic attack.

Today there are many effective therapies and medications for panic attacks. Success rates are so high that if your partner doesn't improve after three or four months of treatment, he would be well advised to look for medical problems underlying his symptoms (Burns 2007).

BEHAVIORAL, COGNITIVE BEHAVIORAL, AND EXPOSURE THERAPY

Behavioral therapy and cognitive behavioral therapy (CBT) are perhaps the most widely used and successful kinds of therapy for panic attacks (Stein 2004). The behavioral approach is based on the idea that panic attacks can be reduced (if not eliminated) by changing a person's behavior—through exercise, deep breathing, meditation, muscle relaxation, and other stress-reducing techniques. (See chapter 7 for additional techniques.) CBT is also based on this idea, and on a second idea: that helping clients view themselves, events, and others more realistically is key, as well.

Many behavioral and cognitive behavioral therapists use exposure techniques (described in chapters 5 and 7). In a controlled way, clients are exposed to situations associated with their panic attacks. They either imagine the situation, view pictures or films or listen to sounds of it (or similar situations), or approach it directly. They do so step by step and at their own pace. They begin by facing the least feared aspect of the situation and then progress to the more feared aspects.

Quite naturally, clients become anxious. But with a therapist's help, they practice various self-calming techniques. For example, after an airline crash, a flight attendant began having panic attacks just thinking about returning to work. First the therapist guided her in using self-calming techniques in response to a picture of a sitting airplane. After the flight attendant succeeded in not reacting fearfully to the picture, she viewed footage of a flying airplane. Her next challenge was to drive to the airport, but not enter it; then to enter it, but not board a plane; then to board a plane for five minutes—then ten minutes, then a half-hour, and so on, until she could resume flying again.

By working through her panic reactions in a controlled, graduated manner, she became increasingly comfortable with flying. Though flying isn't 100-percent safe, she felt safe enough to return to work without fear of having a panic attack.

Dos and Don'ts

Here are some suggestions for helping your partner through a panic attack:

1. Go to a safe place with a toilet (in case he's nauseated or has trouble controlling his bowels). Avoid judgmental others. If you aren't with him, have him locate a supportive person to help him get to a safe place.

2. Don't try to comfort him by touching or putting your arms around him. If he feels pinned down he could become violent. Ask before you touch.

3. Sometimes it helps to hold onto something that's fixed to the ground, such as a fence or a pole. Breathing into a paper bag is commonly viewed as being helpful to people who hyperventilate during panic attacks; however, it's no longer recommended.

4. If your partner wants to go the emergency room, go—even if you don't agree it's necessary.

Perhaps you aren't familiar with what a panic attack looks like. Even if you are, you aren't a doctor. And you could be so distressed by your partner's condition that you can't make a good decision about whether emergency care is needed.

Your partner could be having seizures, for example, which aren't a symptom of panic attacks. Yet you could easily mistake them for the shaking involved in panic attacks. You might also be unaware of some of his symptoms. Perhaps they don't show, or he doesn't mention them, or he says they aren't "that bad."

Therefore, if you have the slightest fear that your partner is having something more than a panic attack (especially if he's having hallucinations, headaches, or other symptoms in addition to panic attack symptoms), or if the episode isn't almost over after ten minutes, call 911 or one of the emergency medical and mental health numbers on your list and get help.

Rage Reactions

Anger is not the same thing as aggression. Anger can be an appropriate response to being mistreated, or a sign that certain improvements are needed in one's life. But sometimes, anger can lead to physically aggressive acts, such as damaging property or hurting someone and to extreme forms of anger called rage reactions.

The "No-Think Zone"

Just as there are different degrees of happiness, there are different degrees of anger. Think of anger as being on a scale of 1 to 10, with 1 being slightly annoyed and 10, ready to commit murder. At 2, you're quite annoyed; at 3, very irritated. By 5, you're noticeably angry and restless. By 6, you're on the verge of saying or doing something you might regret later, but you can stop yourself. By 7, however, you have trouble controlling your urge to lash out destructively.

Somewhere between points 7 and 10, you become so livid you enter what's called a "no-think zone." This means you're increasingly unable to reason or be reasoned with. All you can think about is your anger. And the more you think about it, the more it grows. When others talk, you aren't really listening. All you hear is your anger. You are now in the midst of a rage reaction.

Causes of Anger and Rage

Anger can be caused by hunger, thirst, fatigue, pain, sleep deprivation, and other kinds of physical distress, or by untreated depression, substance abuse, alcohol or drug withdrawal, or any number of medications. It can also result from medical problems, ranging from a simple lack of certain B vitamins to cancer, diabetes, altitude sickness, AIDS, and various heart, lung, thyroid, and liver problems.

Anger can also stem from grief, guilt, jealousy, confusion, frustration, insecurity, feelings of powerlessness, and other emotions.

PTSD and Anger

Like most people, survivors get mad when they feel betrayed, rejected, or powerless. But some survivors, especially those with untreated PTSD or an addiction, tend to get angrier more quickly. One reason is that a survivor's anger may have two levels: the anger belonging to the current situation, and that which belongs to a traumatic event.

For example, when a copy of a key Darnell had made didn't work, he bypassed some of the lesser degrees of anger and flew almost directly into the "no-think zone." Anyone might be annoyed at being locked out of a car. But Darnell's anger was fueled by times when guns and certain other military equipment didn't work. Once, Darnell had tried to pull a buddy out of a burning car, but the key to the vehicle jammed. Darnell's justifiable rage at his buddy's unnecessary death could have easily caused Darnell to curse the locksmith. If Nina had been there, he might've yelled at her too.

Stress and anger. When people are already stressed, something that would usually only annoy them can make them furious. Survivors live under a constant state of biological and emotional stress. This stress increases the chances that their anger will be out of proportion to the situation at hand, especially if they have biochemical imbalances due to the severity of their trauma.

Darnell, who served three tours of combat duty, explains, "I'm like a car that's been driven over rough terrain for thousands of miles with little time for tune-ups and repairs. My brakes don't work well and my shock absorbers are worn out. So every bump in the road feels like a major jolt and makes me mad.

"Nina starts out at point 1 or 2 on the anger scale. But most days I start out at 4 or 5. So it doesn't take much to get me into the 'no-think zone.'"

Anger at PTSD. Survivors can be triggered into anger by something small. But they can also be angry about being triggered, angry at their PTSD, and even angry at themselves for having PTSD. If they feel they have to attend therapy because of their PTSD, they can be angry about that too.

Anger as a "catchall" emotion. Anger has been called a "catchall" emotion. For many people, especially survivors, anger can be a defense against grief, and against feelings of helplessness, guilt, or shame. Feeling angry and full of adrenaline gives one a sense of power. In contrast, sadness, confusion, and fear usually leave one feeling physically and emotionally weak and vulnerable. Hence many survivors would rather be mad than sad.

In some occupations, such as law enforcement and the military, anger is one of the few acceptable emotions. Losing control of anger is usually frowned upon, but anger at enemy forces or at suspected or known criminals is seen as not only permissible, but often desirable. On the other hand, being sad, afraid, or confused on the job could lead to ridicule and possibly dismissal.

Impacted anger. Because their anger is so intense, many survivors try to suppress it for fear of harming someone. It then becomes "impacted." Sarah Haley (1974, 192), known for her PTSD work, describes many of her clients as being caught in the grip of a "paralyzing passivity" because they fear losing control of their anger.

Trying to suppress anger, however, is like sitting on a volcano. No matter how hard one tries to stifle it, it can still erupt. People are often puzzled when a usually controlled or passive mate bursts into rage. Ironically, his very attempts to keep a lid on his anger may have contributed to his outburst.

Helping Prevent Rage Reactions

The following suggestions might help reduce the frequency of your partner's rage reactions. But if he has unresolved anger issues or untreated medical or emotional issues, their effectiveness will be limited.

Nevertheless, using positive communication skills (described in chapters 3 and 4) and helping him manage his triggers (as described in chapter 5) can be beneficial. Also check to see if irritability, anger, restlessness, or insomnia are listed as possible side effects of any of your partner's medications.

It's his responsibility, however, to address the underlying causes of his rage. He also needs to be willing to regularly practice stress-reducing techniques or find other safe ways of lowering his overall level of anxiety and anger. Anger-management classes and self-help books can be helpful, as can certain psychiatric medications specifically designed to help control rage reactions. If you need help expressing or controlling anger, these resources can be useful to you too.

ANTICIPATING RAGE REACTIONS

Be alert for signs that your partner is angry, or that his anger is rising or already at the point of a rage reaction.

Signs of anger. Common signs of anger include muscle tightness, a flushed face, crying, verbal abuse, impatience, clenched fists, frowning, furrowed eyebrows or forehead, darting eyes, shallow or variable breathing, hostile gestures or sounds, restlessness, sweating, hand-wringing, and changes in food habits, energy level, sex drive, or alcohol or drug intake.

Your partner may not show any of these signs, however, even if he's angry. Perhaps during his trauma he, like certain other survivors, learned how to hide his anger. In fact, he may be a master at hiding it because disguising it may have saved his life. So he could be smiling and seemingly calm one minute, and furiously cursing the next.

Signs of rising anger. Signs of rising anger or an upcoming or ongoing rage reaction include:

1. Increasingly shorter, confusing, and irrelevant statements; increased difficulty finding words, completing sentences, or focusing on what you're saying

2. Increased cruelty in the form of verbal attack

3. Increasingly rapid speech and loud tone of voice

4. Pulling at the body: nail biting, picking at scabs, or poking himself with a pencil

5. Reports of losing control in other areas of life, such as eating, drinking, or spending money (especially if such behavior is unusual)

6. Statements indicating that he's no longer committed to the people or values that used to stop him from being violent, or that he no longer fears going to jail or other consequences of violence

7. Talk of suicide, weapons, or violent acts committed in the past, either by him or by others

8. Violent threats toward property, people, or animals

9. Throwing or destroying small objects

10. Seeming out of touch with reality: garbled speech, delusions, hallucinations, or irrational suspiciousness

If he displays any of the signs listed in 7 through 12, or if you're at all afraid, call for help immediately. Take all threats seriously, and follow the recommendations for staying safe in the upcoming section on domestic violence.

DEFUSING RAGE REACTIONS

If help isn't available, or while waiting for help to arrive, try to calm your partner down and buy time. Some suggestions are provided below. Use only those you feel might be helpful.

1. Don't criticize him or tell him what to do. Always offer choices.

2. Approach him only if he asks you to come closer; otherwise, give him space. But don't stand so far away that you need to raise your voice or yell to be heard.

3. Stay (or pretend to be) calm. Have a relaxed posture and tone of voice. Speak and breathe as steadily as possible. Your being emotional could make him more tense or fearful that you might attack him.

4. Ask, "What can I do to help?" or "Would you like me to help you calm down?"

5. Remind him of his inherent worth, your commitment to him, and your faith that you can weather the crisis or disagreement at hand: "I believe that everyone is valuable, including you. When you're angry like this, it's hard on both of us. But I'm sure we can get through this."

6. If he's verbally attacking you, use the suggestions in chapter 3 for active listening and for showing empathy when your partner is being critical. Not lashing back at him isn't "rolling over" or "selling out." It's a chance to exert some control over the situation. Given his state of mind, fighting back might only increase his rage.

7. Suggest a time-out. If he objects, or if you fear that leaving the room would make him angrier, suggest that you both go to another room, go for a walk, or have something to eat or drink together. A change of place or activity could help him cool down.

8. If he's not verbally attacking you, having him talk about his anger could help calm his rage. Consider asking, "How angry are you?" "How long have you been angry about this?" "How angry could you get over this?" "How did you control your anger the last time you were this angry?" or "How would you like the situation to change for the better?"

If you feel that such questions could make him angrier (or angry at you), don't ask them. If he doesn't want to talk, stop asking questions.

9. If any of the above suggestions seem to upset him further, stop using them. Try to get help and get away.

Domestic Violence

Violence must exist in a relationship for it to be considered a battering one. A battered person is not simply one who has a critical or unappreciative partner. She is one who has experienced one or more life-threatening events at the hands of her partner. She knows that he is capable of directing severe blows toward her, and perhaps of ultimately killing her.

Almost any kind of abuse can happen once or twice. But if it happens three times and the partner stays in the relationship, she is usually considered to be battered.

The rage reactions, flashbacks, and nightmares associated with PTSD don't automatically lead to domestic violence. But sometimes they do. This section explains the difference between PSTD-related and non-PTSD-related domestic violence, and provides suggestions for staying safe.

Flashbacks and Intimate Partner Violence

Dramatic cases involving survivors taking hostages or in other ways acting irrationally or violently during flashbacks have been well publicized in the media. Most flashbacks, however, last only a few seconds and occur quietly in the hearts and minds of survivors. If your partner can carry on a conversation or make love, you may not even know that he's "flashing."

Nevertheless, survivors have harmed their partners in the midst of flashbacks. Flashbacks can be conscious or unconscious. During conscious flashbacks, the survivor may or may not be in touch with present-day reality. Yet even if he is in contact with reality, if he's somehow feeling threatened by you (or confuses you with someone who harmed him during his trauma), violence could follow.

During conscious flashbacks, you can try to bring him back to the present by reminding him who you are and where he is now. But during unconscious flashbacks, he's lost in the world of the trauma. In that state, he's more likely to be unreachable, and the chances of violence are greater.

PTSD-Related vs. Non–PTSD-Related Family Violence

Survivors who become violent can be divided into two groups: those whose violence is a direct result of their PTSD and those who would probably have been violent even without PTSD. Some of the violence in the second group may be related to PTSD. Yet the main reason for their abusiveness is a personality problem, a family history of violence, or some other cause. For the purposes of this chapter, this second group will be referred to as "typical abusers," because they are more like typical, nontraumatized abusers than survivors who probably would never have become violent unless they had been traumatized.

PTSD-RELATED FAMILY VIOLENCE

The domestic violence associated with PTSD tends to be sporadic and clearly related to a nightmare, flashback, or other PTSD symptom. Afterward, the survivor is so ashamed and remorseful that he usually withdraws from his partner. He may even decide to leave her rather than risk hurting her again.

Survivors who become violent for PTSD-related reasons usually take full responsibility for their behavior. They don't blame their partners; they blame themselves. They also don't minimize or make excuses for their violence.

THE MANY ASPECTS OF TYPICAL ABUSE

In contrast, a typical batterer usually accuses his partner of exaggerating the violence. And he blames her for it: something she did "provoked" him, so she deserved to be hit.

Afterward, the typical abuser may be sorry, but his remorse is short-lived. Typically, the violence increases over time. What starts as a slap in the face can escalate to burning, cutting, locking up, starvation, denying necessary medical care, and worse.

Domestic violence includes many forms of physical cruelty other than beatings: for example, abandoning a partner in a dangerous place, forcing her to take drugs, or subjecting her to reckless driving. The typical batterer also engages in sexual, spiritual, economic, and social abuse.

In some cases, sexual abuse can involve not only forcing sex, but also withholding sex in order to punish one's partner, insisting that one's partner dress more provocatively than she wants, or publicly flirting with others in order to humiliate her. Spiritual abuse can mean anything from forcing one's partner to do things that go against her spiritual standards to claiming that abusing her serves a spiritual purpose.

The typical abuser also tries to control his partner by taking over the family finances and by restricting her social and other activities. He may also threaten to harm children, relatives, friends, or pets if she doesn't obey him. His need to dominate her isn't related to his PTSD, but to his other issues.

THE MYTH OF HERCULES

In contrast, PTSD-related violence isn't part of a larger pattern of family violence. It includes physical and emotional abuse, but not spiritual, social, sexual, or financial abuse.

Neither PTSD-related violence nor the more typical family violence is excusable. But they are not the same. Hercules, the mythical Greek hero, killed his wife and children because of his PTSD. But he wasn't a wife-beater.

According to the myth, one day Hercules and his wife were watching their children play in a sports event. The physical setting of the game was similar to that of a terrible battle in which Hercules had fought. And the children's rapid movements reminded Hercules of the unpredictable aggressive movements of soldiers during combat. These similarities triggered a severe flashback.

During this flashback, Hercules confused his family with enemy soldiers and killed them. Afterward, he gave up his riches, lived in the wilds, and went to priests looking for a way to repent.

Hercules is well known for killing a lion with his bare hands and for other acts of superhuman courage and strength. What's less known is that his heroic feats were forms of penance for murdering his family during an unwanted flashback.

STAYING SAFE

As Hercules's story shows, whether your partner's violence is PTSD-related or not, you are in danger, and you need to seek safety. Contact your local domestic-violence agency or seek professional help. (See the "Helpful Resources" section for guidance.)

Preventing Typical Domestic Violence

If your partner is a typical batterer, you can't control the violence. He may claim that if you change to his liking, he'll stop. But since he has an inner need to batter, he'll continue no matter what you do.

He needs help not only for his PTSD, but also for his need to batter. Anger management is not enough. He needs a program specifically designed for batterers. And he must attend it out of a sincere desire to change, rather than as a way of making you stay with him. Otherwise, after a brief period of good behavior, the abuse will resume.

Preventing PTSD-Related Violence

PTSD-related violence can be prevented only by PTSD treatment. Has your partner ever become violent during a flashback? If so, at the first sign that he's "flashing," go to another room and lock the door, or go to a safe place—if it's safe to do so. Have an emergency suitcase packed and your car keys, credit cards, and other necessities handy in case you need to—and are able to—get away.

Being alert to the signs of rising anger listed in the previous section can be helpful. But flashbacks and nightmares are unpredictable. Even rage reactions can come without warning. You must, therefore, always be prepared to go somewhere safe—if possible. (See the "Helpful Resources" section for specific resources.)

If your partner is having a nightmare, don't touch him or approach him from behind until he's fully conscious. If you want to interrupt his nightmare, stand a few feet away from the bed and gently call out his name, tell him who you are, or describe your home and family.

If he's assaulted you during a nightmare, you could sleep in another room with the door locked. Take a phone and your list of emergency medical and mental health services with you.

Temporarily leaving your residence in order to be safe doesn't mean you're planning to end your relationship. You're simply protecting yourself. In his irrational state, he may lose control and harm you more than he ever intended. When he realizes what he's done, his remorse could reach suicidal proportions. Like Hercules after his PTSD caused the death of his second wife, he might want to give up on himself and choose to die.

Going to a safe place protects not only you (and your children), but also him. If you try to defend yourself or if others come to your aid, he could be injured. Domestic-violence situations can be emotionally volatile and unpredictable. Since officers are frequently shot while responding to domestic-disturbance calls, they're fully prepared to shoot uncooperative abusers (Walker 2009).

Addiction

Addiction is a worldwide problem. Not just survivors, but people whose lives have been relatively untouched by tragedy misuse mood-altering substances or engage in self-destructive activities. They do so in order to cope with—or rather, avoid coping with—life's challenges, or for recreational reasons. But what begins as entertainment or temporary stress relief can easily become an addiction or a way of life.

Effects on Partners

If your partner has an addiction, you have double trouble in every area of life. From your finances to your sex life, you're dealing not only with PTSD, but also with a devastating problem which, if left untreated, will only increase over time. Like family violence, addiction affects everyone in the family in all kinds of ways. It can lead not only to your partner's early death, but also to ongoing shame, guilt, grief, anger, and fear for you and for others who care about her.

Not only are you deprived of a fully functioning mate, but you must watch someone you love deteriorate. The rising costs of her addiction could also be creating serious financial problems. If her addiction involves illegal activities, you may fear for your own safety, as well as hers.

Perhaps you've tried to separate her addiction from her as a person. But when she's practicing her addiction, she becomes the addiction. This change is very hard to deal with, especially if you don't know whether you're dealing with her personality, her PTSD, or her addiction. Wanting to be supportive, yet not to enable her addiction, can also be confusing.

The good news is that most addicts can be rehabilitated. Often several inpatient stays and a lifelong commitment to some type of recovery effort are needed. The underlying PTSD must also be addressed.

In this section you'll learn about some of the addictions most common among survivors. No suggestions will be given for how to prevent addiction, because there are none. You can be supportive. But, as with PTSD, you can't control or cure your partner's addiction. Neither are you the cause of it. Yet there are some ways of coping that can help.

Substance Abuse and PTSD

Some survivors may have had substance-abuse problems before their trauma but trauma made it worse. Others became addicted during their trauma. Perhaps they were forced to consume these substances by their perpetrators or by peer pressure. Others might not have been aware of, or may not have been able to find, less harmful ways of trying to survive.

Still others became addicted only after their trauma, as a way of medicating their PTSD symptoms, or of trying to control their panic attacks, depression, or anger. A review of available studies indicates that the rates of alcohol and drug abuse are at least a dozen times higher for female rape victims (post-rape) than for untraumatized women (Matsakis 2003). Perhaps it's no accident that Bacchus, the mythological god of wine, was an abused child. He turned to alcohol and drugs after being made homeless by his abusive foster parents.

The Nature of Addiction

Today the term "addict" is used very loosely. People talk about being addicted to everything from exercise to a certain brand of coffee. But enjoying a certain activity so much that you sometimes do it to extremes doesn't mean you're addicted to it. Similarly, many people drink too much at times. But that doesn't mean they are alcoholics.

In trying to decide whether your partner has an addiction, consider the purpose of her behavior and its effects on her, your relationship, and other areas of her life. For example, perhaps you feel that her need for antidepressants makes her "just as bad" as a heroin addict. After all, her body may have become so dependent on antidepressants that stopping them causes severe withdrawal effects.

But why is she taking these pills? To increase her ability to function, or to escape life?

Any prescription or over-the-counter drug can be abused. But when taken as directed, drugs can also help people meet their responsibilities, maintain relationships, and expand their lives. In contrast, abusing legal drugs or taking illegal drugs (or practicing unhealthy eating habits) shrinks a person's life.

Once a person becomes addicted to something, eventually it becomes the center of her life. Her relationships, work, recreational activities, and self-care fall by the wayside.

Types of Addiction

Addictions can be either substance-related or non–substance-related. Substance-related addictions involve physical dependence on a mood-altering substance. Non–substance-related addictions involve the compulsive repetition of a self-destructive behavior.

SUBSTANCE-RELATED ADDICTIONS

Any number of legal and illegal substances can become addictive. They fall into three basic categories: stimulants (such as cocaine, caffeine, nicotine, and methamphetamine), sedatives and hypnotics (such as alcohol, barbiturates, and benzodiazepines), and opiates (such as morphine, codeine, heroin, and methadone). Some people can take these drugs without becoming immediately addicted to them. Much depends on dosage, frequency, genetic factors, and the person's unique body chemistry. Frequent use, however, usually leads to addiction.

Some people abuse more than one drug. They may, for example, use an "upper" to elevate their mood, and then take a "downer" if they become overly stimulated or need to sleep.

Most physical addiction involves increased tolerance—meaning that eventually the body becomes used to a certain level of a substance, and over time, more and more is needed to have the original desired effect. For example, at first it may take only one beer to get a "buzz." But soon it takes two beers, then four, and so forth.

When efforts are made to stop or reduce use of the substance, the withdrawal effects can be physically and emotionally painful and frightening. Without medical care, an addict is likely to resume her addiction in order to stop those withdrawal effects.

The *DSM-5* doesn't consider compulsive overeating, bulimia, or other kinds of food abuse to be addictions. Yet many eating disorder specialists argue that food, like alcohol, can be a mood-altering substance, and that food abuse, like alcoholism, can be a progressive, lifelong, and life-threatening problem. They also argue that certain individuals have a body chemistry that causes them to become physically addicted to certain foods (especially sugar and carbohydrates) the same way alcoholics are physically addicted to alcohol.

NON–SUBSTANCE-RELATED ADDICTIONS

The *DSM-5* recognizes only one non–substance-related addiction: pathological (compulsive) gambling. It does not consider problems such as overspending, hair-pulling, self-cutting and other physically self-injurious behaviors, sexual excesses (commonly referred to as "sex addiction"), excessive Internet gaming, or other compulsively repeated harmful activities to be addictions. Currently these problem behaviors are viewed as issues in need of more research.

Yet some mental health professionals still feel these behaviors are addictions in that some people use these behaviors to manage their negative moods and other life problems without regard for the consequences. Regardless of what formal name is given to these and other injurious behaviors, they should be taken seriously and treatment should be sought.

Detecting Addiction

How can you tell if your partner is a "sex addict," someone with an unusually high sex drive, or a survivor in the midst of an adrenaline surge seeking relief through orgasm? If her drinking binges occur mainly on trauma-related anniversaries, does that mean she's not an alcoholic?

The best way to know if your partner has a particular addiction is for her to be assessed by a qualified mental health professional. Some warning signs of addiction are listed below. Just one sign is not enough. But several suggest a serious problem.

WARNING SIGNS OF POSSIBLE ADDICTION

- Increased use of the substance or time spent in the activity, despite knowing about its negative consequences

- Inability to stop or reduce the behavior without having significant withdrawal symptoms

- Reluctance to face problems caused by the addiction, and other life problems

- Lying, covering up, or otherwise minimizing the extent of the problem behavior

- Mood swings

- Depression, anxiety, and suspiciousness

- Making excuses or blaming others for the addiction

- Social withdrawal, or the opposite—inappropriate friendliness with strangers or increased talkativeness

- Irresponsibility, broken promises, and memory problems

- Poor hygiene, nutrition, and sleeping habits

- Participating in illegal activities, or betraying significant others or cherished values to continue the addiction

Some people become more aggressive when practicing their addictions; others, more inhibited. But all addicts become more anxious and emotionally unbalanced when deprived of their "fix," whether it be chemical or behavioral.

Detecting Alcoholism: The Three Stages

According to Milam and Kechan (1981), alcoholism progresses through three stages. During the first stage, your partner's drinking patterns may not seem that different from those of others. Although she may be drinking more, her functioning doesn't seem to be affected. In fact, her abilities may improve. Perhaps the alcohol is giving her the false confidence and energy she needs to be productive and feel more comfortable around others. It could also be smoothing over her PTSD and any tendencies she has toward depression, panic attacks, or rage reactions.

During the second stage, the physical damage caused by alcohol becomes evident. Her cravings for alcohol increase, and she's less able to control her intake. In this stage you'll see the beginning of mood swings, personality changes, and memory problems. She either loses interest in sex or needs large amounts of alcohol to be interested. When she tries to cut back on her drinking, she has withdrawal symptoms. She then needs to drink to counteract them.

During the third stage, her body is so poisoned by alcohol that her withdrawal symptoms now include convulsions, shaking, mental confusion, difficulty walking, poor motor coordination, extreme suspiciousness, delusions, and perhaps hallucinations. She feels the need to drink more frequently, if not constantly. Her physical and mental deterioration, irritability, and moodiness are obvious to others. But she's still in denial.

Detecting Drug Addiction

Staying in the bathroom or other locked rooms for unusual amount of times, giving up old friends to make friends with other addicts, and inability to keep a job or stay in school are common signs of drug addiction. Addicts often borrow money, ask for pay advances, steal from loved ones, prostitute themselves, or commit crimes to pay for a fix.

However, the symptoms of drug abuse and other behavioral addictions vary from one drug type and one individual to the next.

For more precise definitions of various addictions, their warning signs, and withdrawal symptoms, consult a qualified health professional or written material on the subject.

Coping Suggestions

Here are some suggestions for helping yourself and your partner cope with addiction.

1. Educate yourself. Learn all you can about your partner's addiction by reading or obtaining information about it and the types of treatments currently available. (See the "Helpful Resources" section for sources of information.)

2. Get support for yourself. Check out local support groups for family members of addicts. (See "Helpful Resources" for help finding support groups.) Some groups hold meetings by phone or online. Consider counseling for yourself. You'll need all the support you can find as you face tough decisions, such as how much to help her, or whether or not to report her illegal activities to the police.

3. Perhaps you're unable to—or don't want to—have regular counseling. But at least consider meeting once or twice with an expert in your partner's type of addiction to gain some guidance for the unique aspects of your situation.

4. Check out local rehabilitation centers and programs. If needed, consider out-of-state facilities or programs. You can find information about detox and other recovery programs from health care professionals, hospitals, county and state social service and law enforcement agencies, libraries, or online.

Many addicts have undiagnosed health problems. Therefore you need to find programs that also offer health care or are associated with facilities willing to treat your partner's type of addiction. Ideally the program or facility would also have—or transfer her to—a PTSD program or therapist when she's ready.

5. Encourage your partner to get help. (See chapter 7.) Few addictions can be overcome without some type of assistance. Offer to go with her and participate in any family programs.

6. If she won't seek help, consider a planned professional intervention. But be sure that the intervention is handled by trained specialists.

7. Offer emotional support. Remind her frequently that you love her and will support her recovery efforts as best you can. But there's a difference between loving her and financing her addiction or making excuses for it. Refusing to give her money or to protect her from the consequences of her problem can't stop her addiction. But at least you won't be promoting it.

8. Watch who you talk to about her addiction. Many people are judgmental. Your life is hard enough without being given a guilt trip for loving an addict. Talk about your partner's addiction only with trusted others.

9. Watch yourself for denial. When you first noticed her addiction, you might have been confused or gone into denial. This reaction is normal. Even when the signs became obvious, the pain, shame, and guilt involved in facing the truth might have been so great that you minimized the problem. Or perhaps you blamed circumstances (or yourself), and then redoubled your efforts to help her. Some partners stay in denial until the addiction results in an accident, an arrest, or a financial crisis.

If you were in total denial, you wouldn't be reading this section. But the reality of your partner's addiction can be so devastating that you can easily go in and out of denial.

10. Guard your physical and financial safety. If your partner is putting you and your financial security at risk, take measures to protect your physical safety and your financial assets. Talk to a lawyer about your options regarding taking control of your finances. You may not need to take action now. But you need to be prepared for the possibility that you might have to in the future.

Suicide

When Darnell announced that he'd kill himself by the Fourth of July, Nina went into shock. The idea of losing the man she loved was inconceivable to her.

Where had she gone wrong? she wondered. Hadn't she followed every suggestion she could find about being a supportive partner? She must have done something wrong, she thought, or Darnell wouldn't be talking that way.

"How can I live without him?" she asked herself. But her sadness and fear were mixed with anger. "Why doesn't he love me enough to stay alive for me? After all I've done for him, how dare he leave me!"

Nina tried to shove the idea of losing Darnell out of her mind. Yet she couldn't do so entirely. So she tried to make his life so pleasant that he would forget about suicide. She took on additional responsibilities and agreed to his every request.

But when Darnell caught her searching his face for clues about his state of mind, he stormed out of the house. "I'll kill myself if I want to," he threatened. "And if you tell anyone about my plans, I'll do it in front of you!"

Effects of Suicide Threats on Partners

If your partner has mentioned suicide, you are under enormous pressure. You may not know how seriously to take his threats or what to say to him. Like Nina, you may feel helpless, trapped, abandoned, and afraid. You may also be sacrificing more for your partner than you want to, or walking on eggshells lest you do something that pushes him over the edge.

If you think that he sometimes threatens suicide in order to control you, you may also be angry. Yet you may hesitate to confront him lest he carry out his threat. After all, even people who lie to get their way commit suicide.

In the following sections you'll learn more about suicide and some ways of helping to prevent it until outside help is available. Notice the word "helping." If your partner is determined to kill himself, he will—regardless of what you do or don't do. Even people on suicide watch in psychiatric wards sometimes succeed in committing suicide.

PTSD and Suicide

As of the writing of this book, suicide is the tenth most common cause of death in the United States. People with PTSD are at high risk for suicide, as are others who have a psychiatric diagnosis (Klott 2012).

Most people with a psychiatric disorder don't commit suicide. But two-thirds of those who do have some form of depression. Hence if your partner has both PTSD and depression, he's an especially high suicide risk. The risk is also higher if, in addition to PTSD, he also has another anxiety disorder, bipolar disorder, schizophrenia, an addiction, or a family history of suicide; or if he attempted suicide in the past, lost a parent before the age of twelve, or recently lost a friend to suicide (Klott 2012).

His suicide risk also jumps if he's between the ages of forty and fifty-nine and suffers from cancer, heart disease, Parkinson's disease, or chronic pain. These medical problems can lead to depression, which, in turn, increases the suicide risk (Berman and Pompili 2011),

For some survivors, having to deal with cancer or another major medical problem feels like the last straw. After years of coping with PTSD, they may feel they don't have the inner strength to cope with yet another major life challenge. Also, the physical weakness and confinement of having a serious illness can make them feel more vulnerable and betrayed by life than ever. They may then decide that their only option is to say goodbye to life.

Why People Want to Kill Themselves

Most people who talk about suicide don't really want to die; they want to end their pain. Suicide can be viewed as any of the following:

- A way to simplify life: a one-act solution to life's complex problems

- A way of letting the world (or a particular person or group) know how badly one is hurting

- An act of self-hate or a way of killing off a hated part of oneself—such as one's guilt

- An act of revenge: a way to punish others

- A way of taking control over one's life when feeling suffocated by demands

- A way of joining dead relatives and friends

- A way to find peace by ending the inner chaos caused by PTSD or other problems

- A way of paying for perceived sins or actual criminal acts (as in the story of Hercules)

Helping Prevent Suicide

Your partner may blame you for most of his problems. But no matter how much he thinks—or you think—that you failed him, you aren't responsible for his self-destructive thoughts or actions. However, even if he's in treatment, you may be the first person to whom he reveals his wish to die. And if you live with him, you may be the first to see the warning signs of suicide.

SUICIDE WARNING SIGNS

Some people commit suicide without warning. But often there are warning signs:

1. Statements expressing the wish to die ("If things don't change, I'll kill myself," or "Don't buy me a birthday present. I'll be gone by then") or frequent talk about what people will say or do after the person is dead

2. Writings, drawings, letters, or emails written as if the person is already dead

3. Preparations for death: saying goodbye to people, pets, and places; making a will; giving away possessions; wrapping up unfinished business; planning one's funeral; or buying a one-way ticket to a possible suicide location

4. Signs of increased depression: major changes in mood, eating and sleeping habits, or energy level; disinterest in formerly pleasurable or meaningful activities; memory and concentration problems; feelings of hopelessness or helplessness; outbursts of anger; social withdrawal; and physical weakness

5. Increased substance abuse, gambling, overspending, or other addictive behavior

6. Increased guilt, especially survivor guilt

7. Abruptly dropping out of therapy or a recovery program; not taking psychiatric or other medications without explaining the change; the sudden emergence of, or noticeable increase in, reckless or impulsive behavior or preoccupation with fanatical or cult materials

8. Signs of losing touch with reality: delusions or hallucinations—especially statements that a "voice" or outside force is commanding one to die

The chances of suicide are greater if your partner has a well-thought-out plan or a specific date in mind, rather than a vague wish to die at some undefined time. And there's more cause for alarm if he's already decided how he'll kill himself and has ready access to his means of self-destruction than if he hasn't chosen a method or doesn't have the means of self-destruction nearby.

For example, he's more likely to shoot himself if he already has a gun, or knows where to find one, than if he doesn't have one or hasn't thought much about where to find one. This doesn't mean that people who talk suicide but lack a set plan won't kill themselves. Their warning signs need to be taken seriously too.

Taking Action

If your partner talks about suicide or shows any of the warning signs described above, ask him the following questions:

• Do you want to kill yourself?

• Do you have a plan? What is it?

- How much do you want to die? How much do you want to live?

- Do you have a specific date in mind?

- Is there someone, or something, telling you to kill yourself?

- Are you willing to give me the pills (or the gun, or whatever he's stated as the means of suicide)?

- Can you promise me you won't kill yourself until you talk to a therapist (or family doctor, clergyperson, or some other trained professional)?

Your partner's answers to these questions can help you identify how likely it is that he will hurt himself. But even if he states he was only joking, call a qualified health professional to discuss his statements as soon as you finish speaking with him.

If your partner has a plan and a date, won't give up the means of self-destruction, can't promise not to hurt himself for a short period of time, gives other disturbing answers to any of the above questions, or shows any of the warning signs of suicide listed above, you must not hesitate to seek help. Call a health professional, a suicide crisis line, or 911 immediately.

If necessary, take him to a hospital emergency room. If you can't, find someone who can. Don't leave him alone. Try to get control over any guns, knives, pills, or other means of self-destruction.

Most suicidal people welcome someone taking over and trying to take care of them. The more attention your partner gets from you and others, the better. If he were absolutely sure he wanted to kill himself, he would've already done so. Instead, he decided to live and give out signals about his hopelessness, because he was hoping someone would notice and help him.

If he objects to your efforts, say, "Object all you want. When you say you want to die, I believe you. You matter too much to me to take any chances." Or say, "Suicide is a big decision. You need time to think about it and talk it over with others so you can be sure it's what you really want."

If your partner has violent tendencies, or if he threatens to harm you or others if you try to help, the above suggestions may not be advisable. You will, however, need to talk to a professional about your situation as soon as possible.

You can't handle this crisis on your own. Even if you promised your partner you wouldn't tell anyone about his suicidal plans, you still need to get professional advice. His life is more important than your promise.

Even mental health professionals are allowed to break the code of confidentiality in life-threatening situations such as suicide. If a client is suicidal, they can contact family members, the police, or other responsible authorities. In fact, they are required to do so.

Trusting Your Instincts

You've been advised to ask health professionals for guidance. But you could be given advice that goes against what you feel you need to do to keep your partner safe. For example, the professional may think you're overly concerned about your partner. But you may be more aware of the depth of his distress.

Unfortunately, some health providers are uncomfortable with the idea of suicide. Others are overloaded with clients or don't pay adequate attention to what clients and their family members are saying. Sometimes even the most dedicated assisting professional doesn't notice glaring warning signs of suicide. And some suicidal people pretend to be feeling better than they really are.

Trust your judgment. If you're told that your partner doesn't need to go to the emergency room, but you feel that he does, then take him. If a particular doctor doesn't seem to be taking your partner's condition seriously, find a different one, or a nonmedical authority.

Nina's Story. The night Darnell stormed out of the house, Nina called his therapist immediately. "Darnell just went walking somewhere," she said. "If I jump in my car right now, I can probably catch up with him. But what do I do then?"

The therapist told Nina to do nothing. "I saw Darnell two days ago and he didn't say anything about suicide," he said. "He's making good progress in therapy. Besides, we went over all the warning signs in group. He knows to call me if he's feeling down."

"But he's mentioned suicide twice to me," Nina protested.

"He was probably just upset with you. Don't worry, he'll be fine."

Nina couldn't believe her ears. She and Darnell were paying this therapist top dollar. But now he was telling her to "detach" and stop being a "controlling, interfering wife."

Despite the therapist's warning to "stop acting like a codependent," Nina decided to look for Darnell. But first she called his family. They quickly decided that Darnell's brothers would search for him. Nina would stay at home in case Darnell returned.

Darnell's brothers found him passed out under a tree. He'd started to slit his wrists, but couldn't go through with it. In his condition he could easily have been mugged or assaulted. If Nina hadn't trusted her instincts, Darnell might not be alive today.

Certainly most professionals are not as misguided as Darnell's. So you're not being advised to disregard professional advice in general. But you do need to pay attention to your gut reactions to your partner's condition.

Like Nina, you may also want to involve trusted family members and friends in helping your partner. If he objects, say, "You may decide to kill yourself. But first you're going to have to fight all of us."

Talking to Your Partner About Suicide

Talking about suicide with your partner won't increase the chances of him killing himself; it will decrease them. Many suicidal people want to talk about how bad they feel. His willingness to talk to you is a sign of hope. It's when he won't talk to anyone, or when he's so depressed or disturbed that he can't communicate his despair, that there's a greater risk of suicide.

Perhaps the main reason people don't kill themselves is their love for, or sense of obligation toward, another person (or cause, organization, pet, or deity, or spiritual belief). More than one of my PTSD clients has confessed, "The only reason I'm still alive is because of my partner" (or child, or parent, or sibling, or friend).

"That's an excellent reason," I reply.

As long your partner can stay connected to someone (you, his counselor, or a friend), that means part of him still wants to live. Maybe 98 percent of him wants to die. But the 2 percent of him that wants to live could pull him through.

Some Dos and Don'ts

Don't deny your partner's suicidal wishes by saying, "You don't mean it," "You'll feel better after dinner," or "You're just mad because we didn't have sex last night." Don't discount his reasons for wanting to commit suicide, either ("It's not that bad," "There you go complaining again, just because things aren't perfect." "You just want me to baby you.").

As frightening or heartbreaking as it may be, let him talk about the part of him that wants to die. Then listen, using every active listening skill and every ounce of empathy you can muster. You could say, for example, "You're in so much pain!" or "Things are so bad for you! How do you stand it?" or "I can see why you feel hopeless." (See chapter 3 for more on active listening and communication skills.)

Consider asking him what it feels like to have suicidal thoughts: "What's it like to not be sure if you want to live or die?" or "What's it like to want to die but still be alive?"

Additional Suggestions

You can't be your partner's therapist. But you may feel as if you've been forced to act like one when you're alone with him and he mentions suicide, especially during a suicide crisis.

The suggestions provided below, and by other recommended books or qualified health professionals, may or may not be helpful. Since you know your partner's personality, what matters to him, and what doesn't, you'll need to decide which approaches might encourage him, or at least buy time.

"Don't try to convince him to stay alive, or tell him his reasons for living," more than one self-help book, website, or therapist has emphasized. Yet you may sense that your mate feels so worthless, defeated, mentally disoriented, confused, or physically exhausted that he needs to be reminded about what he'd be leaving behind.

Partners are also usually told not to moralize or shame the person in crisis by calling him a sinner or a coward for thinking about suicide. Yet sometimes appealing to a survivor's religious beliefs or his sense of honor has been effective. Once, a suicidal veteran said to me, "Stop being so nice! Why don't you just say that killing myself means I'm a chicken and an irresponsible father? Yell at me, please. Then maybe I'll listen."

Regardless of which approach you choose, pay attention to your partner's responses. If a particular approach makes him upset or withdrawn, or makes him think that you don't understand his feelings, drop it.

Don't limit yourself to the suggestions provided below or elsewhere. Use your knowledge of your partner and your creativity to speak from your heart to the one you love.

1. Ask him who he thinks might miss him if he were gone, and to recall his positive experiences with these people. If he's not capable of doing this, then say the names of these people (or pets, or organizations, or whatnot) aloud. Remind him of the positive things these people have said about him, and his good times with them. Find photographs of these people and put them in obvious places.

2. Tell him that if he kills himself you'll be very, very sad for a very long time. You'll carry on, but you'll miss him terribly.

3. If his suicidal purpose is revenge, ask him if his death will really serve to punish. Will the person he wants to punish really feel sorry about what she did? If she does feel guilty, how long will she feel guilty? If she didn't care about him when he was alive, why would he think she'll care about him when he's dead? Might she be glad he's gone? Could she use his suicide as proof that he was 'crazy' or 'bad,' and that therefore she was right to have mistreated him? Encourage your partner to find safer ways of seeking compensation.

4. If he wants to kill himself because he feels worthless, you could say, "Feelings aren't facts. Just because you feel worthless, doesn't mean you are. You keep saying you're a nothing. But you must feel you're worth something or you wouldn't be talking to me right now. If I thought you were worthless, I and others wouldn't care about you the way we do."

5. If he sees his future as nothing but an endless rerun of his past miseries, you could say, "You don't know that. For all you

know, things could get worse. But they could also improve. Nobody knows the future. But I do know that your story isn't over—and that there's always hope and always something that can be done to make things better."

6. Emphasize that suicidal thoughts and feelings of worthlessness and hopelessness are caused by a medical condition called depression, and that it's highly treatable. Then discuss getting help. (See chapter 7.)

    If he's already getting help, perhaps he needs a different kind of help, or a different therapist. Or perhaps he needs medication, or his medication needs to be reevaluated. Sometimes medications lose their effectiveness or have a rebound effect that makes matters worse. Or he may have developed a medical condition that hasn't been identified. Hence another complete physical may be in order.

    Offer to do any needed research, make any necessary appointments, and go with him. Don't worry about doing "too much" for your partner or making him dependent on you. You're in the middle of a crisis. You therefore need to do every reasonable thing possible to help. After the crisis has passed, you can resume a more balanced relationship.

7. Encourage him by asking him what he did the last time he was stressed (or suicidal). What's the same and what's different? How is this time worse? Does he have anything going for himself now that he didn't have then?

8. Ask if any of his family members or friends have ever had hard times. What kept them going? Did any of them ever want to commit suicide? Why didn't they? If they did, why did they? How does he feel about their actions? What would he tell you if you wanted to commit suicide?

9. If you have children, remind your partner that his suicide will teach them that suicide is the way to handle life's problems. Since the suicide of a loved one—especially a parent—is considered a trauma, he could also cause them PTSD.

   At the very least, they'll go through life feeling abandoned by their father, blaming themselves for his death, and wondering why he didn't love them enough to stay alive for them. If he feels like he's not a good father, say, "Even a not-so-good father is better than no father."

   On the other hand, if you feel that talking about the effects on your children or others might feel like a guilt trip or make your partner angry, then don't.

10. Mention that not all suicide attempts are successful. He could end up disabled.

If You Have an Emotional Outburst

Partners have fallen on their knees and begged their mates not to kill themselves. Others have cursed them or threatened to commit suicide themselves if they commit suicide. Still others have broken all the rules of empathy and said things like, "You're so selfish! Do you know what killing yourself would do to me and everyone who cares about you?" "What kind of husband are you, anyway?" or "You hypocrite! What happened to your faith in God?"

In a desperate effort to prevent your partner's suicide, you may say something hurtful or make threats. This is normal. If it happens, as quickly as possible explain that you didn't know what else to say to let him know how much he means to you.

As grim as the subject of suicide may be, keep in mind that sometimes it takes a suicide crisis to convince a person to get the help he deserves. The overwhelming majority of people who kill themselves have a psychiatric disorder for which they never sought help (Klott 2012). So getting help is perhaps the best form of suicide prevention.

In the following chapter, you'll learn about different kinds of trauma therapy, ways of encouraging your partner to seek help, and ways of helping yourself heal from the stress of living with someone with PTSD.

CHAPTER 7

PTSD Therapy and You

An ancient myth describes a magic potion that made warriors forget their anger and grief. It worked only for a few hours, but soldiers traveled days just for a sip of it.

We all wish for a magic potion, or person, capable of taking away our pain. Perhaps your partner hoped, or still hopes, that you would be her magic rescuer. Perhaps, on some level, you also feel, or felt, that your love could heal her wounds.

Love is essential, but sometimes it's not enough. Your partner also needs the help of a qualified PTSD therapist. Support groups can be helpful too. And sometimes medication is needed, as well.

This chapter discusses medication for PTSD, the different kinds of PTSD therapy, and how your partner's therapy could affect you and your relationship. It also offers suggestions for encouraging your partner to get help—and for helping you recover from the stress of living with someone with PTSD.

Medication

There is no "PTSD pill." But antidepressant and antianxiety medications can help manage the anxiety, depression, and other symptoms associated with PTSD. Medication should be aimed at the symptoms causing the most problems. For example, if insomnia prevents your partner from concentrating at work or in therapy, then sleep medication should be a priority. In some cases medication is needed only for a short time; in others, for a lifetime.

Medication Difficulties

Sometimes medication provides almost immediate relief. But medications don't always work right away—and they all have side effects. Their side effects need to be weighed against their benefits. It may be necessary to try several different types or doses of medications before the right amount of the right drug (or combination of drugs) is found. This process takes considerable patience on the part of the survivor and considerable monitoring on the part of the psychiatrist.

There are also racial and ethnic differences in the effects of certain medications. Since most research on psychiatric drugs is based on Caucasians, survivors from other groups may experience more frustrations in finding the right medication. Women from all groups may experience similar frustrations because the interactions of female hormones and psychiatric medications have not been adequately studied.

The Limits of Medication

Medication is useful. But it only treats symptoms. It can't help survivors accept or learn from their trauma. One of the talk therapies described below will also be necessary.

The warriors who drank the magic potion eventually had to go back home and face their problems. But the magic potion gave them the temporary relief they needed to make it home and begin rebuilding their lives. Similarly, medication gives some survivors the boost they need to benefit from counseling and otherwise help themselves.

Who Can Prescribe Medication

Any physician can prescribe psychiatric medication. But it's usually best to have your partner assessed for medication by a psychiatrist familiar with PTSD. Talk therapy for PTSD can be conducted by psychiatric nurses, social workers, marriage and family therapists, and psychologists. But only psychiatrists can prescribe medication. Unlike other therapists, psychiatrists have completed medical school and have an MD degree. Some also provide talk therapy.

Levels of PTSD Therapy

There are two levels of PTSD therapy: symptom management and trauma processing. Some survivors require or desire only symptom management. Others want or need both.

Symptom Management

The level of trauma therapy called symptom management focuses on teaching survivors coping skills that can help them gain some control over their symptoms. For example, by mastering self-calming techniques, survivors can prevent anxiety from growing into a state of unmanageable hyperarousal. They can also learn how prevent anger from turning into rage reactions, and feelings of depression from becoming long periods of deep despair.

Increased control over symptoms helps some (but not all) survivors participate in activities that used to trigger them so much that these activities used to be avoided. It can also give some survivors the freedom to feel feelings they used to fear might overwhelm them. Consequently they come to feel safer within themselves and, therefore, safer around others.

For some survivors, increased control over their symptoms is enough to help them move on. The past is still with them. But they can begin taking steps toward building a new life without reviewing their trauma in depth.

In sum, the goal of symptom management is to help survivors do these three things:

1. Increase control over their symptoms in order to reduce the need to organize their lives around avoiding triggers

2. Improve their self-esteem

3. Improve their relationships by learning how to stay connected to others even when they're triggered

Trauma Processing

Some survivors also want to talk about their trauma (or at least certain key events) in depth so they can better understand what happened. Or perhaps they need to do so before they can handle certain triggers, especially long-standing ones.

This level of trauma therapy, in which the past is revisited and examined, is called trauma processing. It usually involves putting together the story of one's trauma, trying to make sense of what happened, and examining the impact of the trauma on one's current life. Some survivors also try to put their trauma into some kind of spiritual or existential framework.

Trauma processing therapy always involves symptom management as well. Without some degree of control over her symptoms, a survivor cannot safely face her past.

In sum, trauma processing includes the goals of symptom management described above. It can also help a survivor achieve one or more of the following goals:

1. Recall enough of her trauma so she understands why she feels so bad

2. Examine her trauma rationally in hopes of reducing unfounded self-blame and improving her self-esteem

3. Help her face and express suppressed emotions associated with the trauma so that they don't dominate her life

4. Find some meaning or purpose in her suffering, or accept not being able to find any

Quite often during trauma processing, "it gets worse before it gets better." If your partner revisits her past in depth, her symptoms may temporarily worsen. She may become increasingly agitated, depressed, or unavailable to you. This is a necessary stage, however, toward becoming better able to reconnect with herself and others. If her symptoms continue to get worse, ask to speak to the therapist. Additional help or a different kind of help may be needed.

Realistic Expectations

Notice that none of the above goals include forgetting the past or eliminating all PTSD symptoms. Such goals are biologically impossible. Your partner's trauma will continue to affect her. But with sufficient competent help, it will no longer be the major focus of her life.

Therapy can also help your partner be more honest and handle her emotions and relationships more constructively. But therapy isn't a "cure-all." It can't promise a pain-free or anxiety-free existence. Nor can it protect either you or your partner from the hardships of life or from future painful emotions and conflicts.

Your partner's individual therapy may not be enough to address your relationship issues. Couples counseling or family therapy, and perhaps sex therapy, may also be needed. (See "Helpful Resources.")

Kinds of Therapy

Several kinds of talk therapy have proven to be helpful to survivors. But no one treatment works for everyone. Your partner may need to try different approaches until she finds one that works for her.

Cognitive Behavioral Therapy

Cognitive behavioral therapy (CBT) is the most widely used and recommended form of trauma therapy (Regel and Joseph 2010). The basic ideas behind this approach were described in chapter 6, in the section on treating panic attacks. In treating PTSD, these same ideas (such as learning to view oneself, events, and others more realistically) are used to help survivors improve their mood and behavior and cope with triggers. For example, some survivors, due to their trauma, believe they must be perfect to be loved. Or perhaps they tend to focus on the fearful aspects of a situation rather than the situation as a whole. Cognitive behavioral therapists help survivors recognize and correct these and other mistaken ways of thinking.

Like behavioral therapists, they also help survivors reduce their anxiety and depression by teaching them any number of stress-reducing methods, such as muscle relaxation and deep breathing, or by using exposure techniques (described in chapters 5 and 6) or the techniques used in mindfulness, Acceptance and Commitment Therapy, and other therapies described below.

Eye Movement Desensitization and Reprocessing

In the therapeutic method called Eye Movement Desensitization and Reprocessing (EMDR), clients are asked to move their eyes back and forth while thinking about some aspect of their trauma. EMDR also includes talking about the traumatic event and their feelings about it. The goal is to process distressing memories, reduce their lingering effects, and help the client develop more adaptive coping mechanisms.

Although the reasons it works are still being debated, EMDR has given many survivors a sense of peace about their trauma. But EMDR doesn't work for everyone. Similarly, hypnosis helps some survivors, but not all (Regel and Joseph 2010).

Acceptance and Commitment Therapy

Acceptance and Commitment Therapy (ACT) attempts to help people face and accept their emotional pain and their other current life problems without being paralyzed by them. Unlike CBT, ACT doesn't try to change or stop undesirable thoughts and feelings. Instead it encourages people to define themselves in terms of their values rather than their problems or their past. Through a variety of exercises, people are helped to develop a fulfilling life by defining their values and developing a plan for acting on them.

Dialectical Behavior Therapy

Dialectical Behavior Therapy (DBT) is a highly structured form of therapy. It teaches skills for managing uncomfortable emotional reactions (such as anxiety, anger, and feelings of abandonment, hopelessness, and worthlessness). DBT also teaches interpersonal skills— for example, learning how to say no, ask for what one wants, and handle conflicts constructively. Some of these skills resemble those taught in positive communication, assertiveness, and conflict-resolution classes and self-help books.

By learning a variety of coping skills, survivors are better able to handle emotional distress. As a result they may be able to face situations they used to avoid.

Mind–Body Therapies

The mind-body connection is especially important in healing from trauma. Behavioral therapy and CBT use muscle relaxation and other self-calming methods that rely on the mind-body connection. The term "mind-body therapy," however, usually refers to approaches such as mindfulness therapy and energy tapping.

Mindfulness therapy combines elements of yoga and Buddhist meditation. It directs survivors to focus on their breathing and the present moment, and to observe their thoughts and feelings rather than judge them. Energy tapping involves gently tapping (or imagining tapping) on various acupressure points while repeating positive statements about eliminating the cause of the distress.

These and other mind-body therapies, such as acupuncture and yoga, can help lessen anxiety and depression.

How Therapists Differ

CBT, EMDR, ACT, DBT, and the other mind-body therapies listed above are all techniques that can help survivors manage their symptoms. If a therapist and a client agree that the client is ready, any one or more of these techniques can be used as a springboard for revisiting the trauma in depth.

On the other hand, some therapists (or therapy programs) focus primarily on, or limit their treatment to, symptom management and helping clients apply these skills to their present-day problems. In other words, if a survivor brings up a traumatic incident, the therapist encourages her to focus more on managing her reactions to the incident than on further describing or analyzing it. Hence clients who want or need to discuss their past in greater depth may need to continue treatment with a therapist who is qualified and willing to do trauma processing.

Some therapists use only one kind of technique or approach. Others combine various techniques and approaches. Some therapists skilled in CBT, ACT, or some other method also offer trauma processing. Others do not, or only to a limited degree. Most existential and expressive therapists (described below) provide both symptom management and trauma processing.

Existential and Expressive Therapies

Existential therapy helps people find meaning and purpose in their trauma through talking about their experience and their values. For many people, though, trauma can create feelings that can't be put into words. And some aspects of trauma are stored nonverbally as images or body sensations.

Expressive therapies use drawing, dance, music, and other art forms to help survivors get in touch with and express aspects of their trauma that cannot adequately be put into words.

For further information about these and other PTSD treatments, see the "Helpful Resources" section.

Addiction and Self-Injury Recovery vs. Trauma Recovery

Twelve-step programs (such as Alcoholics Anonymous, Narcotics Anonymous, and Overeaters Anonymous) and private addiction rehabilitation programs have save thousands of lives. But their purpose is overcoming an addiction, problem eating, or other self-destructive behavior—not recovering from trauma.

Your partner's addiction (or other self-injurious behavior) and her PTSD may be closely related. But they aren't the same. So she'll need both a trauma recovery program and an addiction recovery program, or one specifically designed for her form of self-injury. However, trauma therapy can't be attempted if she's actively practicing her addiction or self-injurious behavior. She must first receive help for the addiction or other problem behavior.

The Nature of Healing

People who can express their emotions tend to make faster progress in trauma therapy. But even they have setbacks. Setbacks are normal. When getting over the flu, for example, you may feel better for a few days, but then some symptoms may return. A setback doesn't mean you'll never get well; it means that the body isn't a machine that, once fixed, stays fixed.

The human psyche isn't a machine either. At times your partner may seem to be taking three steps forward, then two steps backward. Don't be alarmed. She's still making progress. Setbacks usually occur because of additional life stresses or illness. Or perhaps your partner has been revisiting more of her trauma in therapy than she can handle, or going farther with exposure therapy than she is prepared to. A setback can be a way of giving herself time to recover from the emotional overload and digest the new material she's uncovered.

If Your Partner Doesn't Improve

Setbacks are temporary. But what if your partner's relapse persists, she doesn't improve, or she seems to be getting worse?

Perhaps she needs a different kind of therapy or a different therapist. If she isn't taking medication, consider it. If she is, it may need to be changed. Or perhaps she was misdiagnosed by one of her health care providers. She may have additional psychiatric or medical conditions that weren't originally detected, or that developed since she was first diagnosed.

If your partner doesn't improve despite these efforts, she may be one of those unfortunate souls who waited too long to get help. Or perhaps help wasn't available until the negative patterns associated with PTSD became part of her personality. Even though therapy may not seem to be helping, it may be keeping her from getting worse or suicidal. Given that some severely traumatized people literally disappear into remote areas of the country, staying the same is no small accomplishment.

There are also some people who were traumatized at such a young age, or so often, by a trusted adult that they have trouble bonding with a therapist. Yet without a positive client-therapist bond, therapeutic progress is difficult, if not impossible. Progress is also difficult for survivors with major medical problems, or those who use therapy to manipulate others or for personal gain.

When Trauma Processing Is Not Advisable

If your partner is under significant stress—for example, if she's being harassed at work or a family member is seriously ill—she may not benefit from trauma processing. Examining her trauma while also coping with a current crisis could cause her to shut down or develop other symptoms.

Some survivors of massive traumas (such as concentration camps, torture, or genocide) may be better off not reviewing their trauma at all. Sometimes trauma processing can make these survivors worse, not better. They may profit more from general supportive counseling, medication, or symptom-management therapies focusing on the present—such as mindfulness or ACT.

Finding a Therapist

The success of your partner's therapy depends on two factors: a positive relationship with the therapist and the therapist's abilities. If your partner isn't comfortable with a therapist, she won't be able to open up in therapy. The therapist needs to be warm, supportive, and respectful. There also needs to be a mutual positive feeling between your partner and the therapist.

At the same time, the therapist must be knowledgeable about PTSD and competent in the specific techniques to be used in the course of therapy. Competence means more than having had a few hours of training or having read a book on the technique. Therapists who conduct trauma processing need to have had special training in trauma processing—beyond attending a few workshops or reading a few books. They also need to be familiar with the specific kind of trauma your partner experienced, or be willing to learn about it.

You and your partner have the right to ask which approaches and techniques a therapist uses and why. You also have the right to inquire about the therapist's credentials and background in PTSD, and in the approach and techniques to be used. Unfortunately, some mental health professionals (including psychiatrists) still doubt the reality of PTSD. Avoid any mental health professional who minimizes the role of trauma in your partner's life. (See "Helpful Resources" for guidance in finding a therapist for you or for your partner.)

Encouraging Your Partner to Seek Help

The following ideas for encouraging your partner to seek help are suggestions only. Since you're more familiar with your partner than this author, you need to screen them. Use only those ideas you feel might be helpful.

Attitude, Tone, and Timing

Suggesting to your partner that he needs help is a delicate matter. No matter how carefully you choose your words or how lovingly you speak them, you're still basically saying that that you think there's something wrong with him. Consider how *you'd* feel if someone suggested that *you* need therapy.

Avoid critical or triggering statements (such as "You're crazy!") and other communication pitfalls described in chapter 3. Your tone can be serious, but not angry, scolding, or condescending. What you say (and how you say it) should not imply that you think he's a "mental case." Instead, your message needs to be that you see him as a responsible, capable person—someone who wants to be a good partner (or parent, or worker, or friend) and who, when he sees a problem, wants to fix it.

If his job required learning new skills, he'd take the necessary training, wouldn't he? Similarly, counseling is a way to learn new skills to handle certain problems. It's not a condemnation of his character or a punishment for some misdeed.

Avoid bringing up the topic of getting help while arguing or when one of you is sick or stressed. Don't pair your appeal with threats, such as that you'll leave him if he doesn't get help. Someday you may have to say that (hopefully not!). But don't make threats the first few times you mention getting help.

Emphasize that you aren't blaming *all* your relationship problems on his PTSD, and that you aren't going to nag him about getting help. You might bring up the subject again, but only once or twice. You might also provide him with some educational materials and contact information for available help. After that, you plan to stop. If his symptoms worsen, however, you may need to mention counseling again, because you care about him.

Indicate that you're willing to be supportive—for example, by taking over some chores or giving up certain personal luxuries to help cover the additional expense. But don't take on too much extra work, and don't be the only one making sacrifices. It's best to find ways you both can economize or extend yourselves in order to make counseling possible.

Work with Your Partner's Values

What does your partner value—being a loyal member of a work team, an involved parent, or an active participant in a particular group, sport, or community effort? What standards does he try to live up to or admire in others— competency, persistence, physical strength, self-control?

List the activities and qualities that matter to him. Then ask yourself how his PTSD might be interfering with his ability to pursue any of these activities or live up to standards he values. You could also consider the ways his PTSD is hurting him. But if you feel your partner, like many survivors, feels undeserving of help, you might have a better chance of reaching him if you focus on how his PTSD is harming others, his sense of duty, or some other aspect of his moral code.

Follow the guidelines in chapter 4 in order to present your thoughts about the negative effects of his PTSD in ways least likely to alienate him.

Consider whether any of his problems could be presented as the continuation of a valuable pattern that helped him survive his trauma, but which may not be as helpful in present-day, less stressful situations. Mention any positive aspects of his problem area. Show empathy for the stress he might have to tolerate in order to change.

For instance, if his need for everything to be neat and clean interferes with helping the children with their homework, you could say, "Overseas you needed to know exactly where everything was because spending time searching for a weapon or tool could have cost you or someone else their life. If I were a soldier, I'd want to be in a unit with someone as organized as you. Whenever there's a power failure, you know exactly where the flashlights are—and they're always in working order because you check them regularly. I really appreciate that and I love not having to pick up after you!

"But there's something else that's important now: the children. You do so much for them and they know you love them. But when you show up an hour late for homework time, they worry about you and feel like they're burdening you. I know how much you enjoy helping them. I also know how stressful it is for you to leave things messy. Maybe counseling can help you with the stress of leaving things undone in order meet the children on time."

If he values being independent and in control, explain that counseling can help him become more self-reliant and have more control over his reactions. Emphasize that even though a counselor can offer suggestions and support, *he'll* be doing most of the work, *not* the counselor.

Focus on Specific Problem Areas

If the very words "PTSD" or "counseling" might cause your partner to storm off or shut down, don't use psychological terms. Instead, focus on specific problem areas, such as communication skills, memory lapses, parenting, or anger or stress management. Use words like "workshop," "class," "course," or "training," instead of "counseling" or "therapy." But be sure the kinds of programs you're suggesting are available and are listed as skills training rather than psychotherapy.

If he's totally against counseling, consider a coach. Today numerous individuals offer help with everyday life problems, from gardening to preparing résumés. Coaches provide moral support for achieving a specific, limited goal. But they aren't equipped to handle deep emotional issues, much less PTSD.

Nonetheless, your partner may find working with someone not associated with the mental health field less threatening than seeing a doctor or therapist. Having a positive experience receiving help on a relatively minor issue might make him more open to seeking help with a qualified trauma specialist. Perhaps your partner will realize that getting help will make him stronger, not weaker; more masterful, not more dependent.

CAUTION

Check the credentials and references of any coach you consider. Currently most coaches are not licensed or regulated by state or national law. Also, if coaches venture beyond their limited sphere of competence, they could do more harm than good.

Address Prior Negative Experiences

Does your partner know someone who had a negative experience with therapy? If so, explore the similarities and differences between that person's problems and circumstances and those of your partner. Mental health issues are all unique, and there are many more types of mental health treatments available today than years ago.

Did he have a negative experience himself? If so, perhaps the therapist wasn't well trained in PTSD or in the techniques being used. Today, many more mental health professionals are trained in trauma work.

Use a Scientific Approach

Use what you've learned about fight-flight-freeze reactions to describe PTSD to your partner in terms of biochemical reactions and imbalances. Outline some of the possible health problems caused by the increased heart rate and other physical aspects of reacting to triggers—for example, high blood pressure.

Talk about how suppressed anger, grief, and guilt can contribute to stress-related illnesses, weaken the immune system, and worsen any existing medical issues. But don't mention this mind-body connection if your partner might resent your suggestion that he has suppressed emotions.

Use External Authorities and Trusted Others

Your partner may resist seeing a therapist. But he might go see a physician. Explain that he could be suffering from a medical problem that's aggravating his PTSD, or maybe he's just suffering from symptoms similar to PTSD but doesn't have PTSD at all!

If he's experiencing some of the medical consequences of PTSD, the doctor might suggest counseling or some form of stress management. Your partner might be more open to counseling if the idea doesn't come from you, but from someone else he respects and admires: a priest, rabbi, or other spiritual leader; or a friend or coworker who has undergone counseling.

Do you have a child who is affected by your partner's PTSD? If so, try to arrange a conference with the school counselor to discuss how family tensions might be harming your child's school performance or mental health. Such a meeting could be a stepping stone toward future counseling with a trauma specialist.

Acknowledge the Hassles

Acknowledge the hassles involved in finding the right therapist and the limits of counseling. Don't present counseling or any other form of treatment as a "magic cure." If your partner has been severely traumatized, there's no quick fix for his pain. And he can easily feel insulted by the implication that his suffering can simply be "talked away."

Instead you could say, "I know counseling isn't a cure-all. Even finding a counselor you like, who understands you and understands PTSD, can be difficult. You might have to interview three or four therapists until you find the right one.

"Then you'll need to wait until you've built trust with the counselor before you can actually start working on anything. But it's worth the time and effort if it helps you even a little bit.

"Counseling can't give you back what you lost, or get rid of the memories. But it can help lighten the load and help you find ways of making your life better. After all you've been through, don't you think you deserve to at least try to see if there's something you can do about some of the things that trouble you? You can always quit if it's not helpful.

"My friend Sue is still angry about that car accident. But counseling helped her think about what she could do in spite of losing her legs. She ended up taking accounting classes online. Now she's a CPA. That's what good counselors do: they help you figure out what you can do despite the things you can't change."

If your partner feels he can't speak freely to a counselor paid by his employer, suggest getting help outside the system.

Address the Fear of Entrapment

Emphasize that counseling isn't a lifetime commitment. All you're asking him to do is go for one fifty-minute consultation. He can leave at any time. And many therapists offer short-term treatments with the option of additional sessions.

Explain that unless he is suicidal or homicidal, he can't be hospitalized or medicated against his will. Even if medication is recommended, he doesn't have to take it. Sometimes medication is suggested only as a temporary measure to help someone through a particularly rough period of time. If he takes the medication and it doesn't help, or it has negative side effects, he can always inquire about alternatives, such as acupuncture, therapeutic massage, improved nutrition, or an exercise program.

Emphasize that he has choices, not only in terms of a therapist, but also in terms of the level and kind of treatment he receives. Often there are different treatments available for a specific problem. A good therapist can explain these alternatives and help him select the type of treatment that might work best. He can always obtain second and third opinions, read self-help books or other materials, or attend classes on a specific topic.

Additional Suggestions

If he still refuses to seek help, ask at what point he would think it time to do so. In *his* opinion (not your opinion or a professional's opinion), what thoughts or behaviors on his part would indicate beyond a doubt that he needed help? If he can't answer this question in terms of himself, ask him to answer it in terms of you or someone else he cares about: "What would you have to see me (or a coworker or relative or friend) doing or thinking in order for you to decide help was needed?"

As a last resort, ask him to go just one time, for your sake. Or ask him to attend one session with you (or another person he loves). Perhaps it can be a start toward reducing his fears about counseling.

Starting Over

You may have waited many years for your partner to start some kind of therapy. You may also have understood why trauma recovery could take a long time. Yet you might have grown weary waiting for improvements.

Finally your partner begins changing in desirable ways. Now, however, you may be concerned about how his progress might affect your routines—and perhaps your feelings about each other as well.

In some ways you're starting over. This can be exciting, yet somewhat scary too.

Shifts in the Balance of Power

While your partner was struggling with PTSD, perhaps you had to make certain important decisions on your own instead of as a couple. He may have felt proud, and relieved, that you could take care of matters. But now that he's more whole, he may want to be more active in family decisions. Or perhaps he used to try to dominate decision making because of his PTSD. But now that he has a more balanced view of life, you can have more power and authority in the home.

Yet one or both of you may be unclear about how you'd like things to change. There may be tension about how much say each of you will now have in important matters. Even if you're both in agreement, at first there may be confusion about who is responsible for what. Such changes can't be made quickly or without some error and flare-ups.

Confronting Relationship Issues

You may have held some things in for years because of your partner's PTSD. Now that he's more able to talk about relationship problems, you may find that you have a backlog of grievances to discuss.

Yet you may hesitate to interfere with his progress by "stampeding" him with all your concerns. At this point you may need to seek help for yourself, or couples counseling (if you haven't done so already.)

This transition into a new phase in your relationship is a delicate one. Handle it with the care it deserves. After all the effort you and your partner have put into your relationship, you're entitled to enjoy the fruits of your labor.

Healing for You

As your partner grows stronger, you may become increasingly aware of the parts of yourself that you set aside for his sake. This growing awareness can lead to strong feelings of anger, grief, guilt, and other emotions. Don't face them alone. Get support.

Developing a Support System

Supportive others can help you cope with the crises created by your loved one's tragic history, and the times when he's not emotionally available to you. Your support system can include members of your family, various organizations, neighbors, a therapist, or a therapy or support group. (See "Helpful Resources" for guidance in finding a therapist.)

Building a support system takes time and commitment. Given your many responsibilities and your partner's PTSD, making the effort to establish one can be difficult. But having support is essential. Just as your survivor can't do it alone, neither can you.

The Importance of Self-Care

Due to space limitations, this book has focused on helping you help your survivor to survive his PTSD. Several more chapters could have been written on helping *you* survive your partner's PTSD. Yet there are many books available on self-care, building self-esteem, and stress management. (See "Helpful Resources.") And, if you Google the terms "home stress," "work stress," or "caretaker stress," you'll find countless websites with suggestions and resources.

These resources may or may not be helpful. But they're definitely worth considering. To the extent that you've taken care of your partner rather than yourself, your immune system and emotional resources have been taxed. There's ample evidence that caretaking can be extremely emotionally and physically depleting (Quittner and Schultz 1998).

It's important, therefore, that you try to take care of yourself as well as your partner. Pay careful attention to the self-care plan you developed in chapter 5. Try to follow it as best you can. You may not be able to make your needs the single most important priority in your life. Nor will you always be able to meet both your needs and those of your loved ones at the same time. But it's still important to find ways of improving your situation, however small these ways may seem.

At the very least, try to recognize all that you do, even when others do not fully acknowledge or appreciate your efforts.

In Closing

This book has described some of the relationship problems that can result from PTSD. It's important to know, however, that a fulfilling relationship with a survivor is possible. In fact, once you and your partner establish positive communication, you may have an even more rewarding relationship than couples who haven't taken the time to learn how to communicate their feelings, values, and personal limitations. And in those instances when survivors are able to accept and grow from their pain, their love for their partner often intensifies.

Much perseverance is required, and there are major difficulties, such as triggers. Yet the rewards of being with a survivor can be enormous. At the end of all your struggles to understand each other's needs, the two of you will be closely bonded, like comrades in arms. Indeed, you'll have fought a kind of war together—a war against ignorance, misunderstanding, selfishness, and needless self-sacrifice, and against the ghosts of the past. You will also have prevented a crippling mental disorder from destroying human love.

Helpful Resources

Addiction: Alcohol and Drug Abuse and Gambling

Organizations and Websites

Al-Anon Family Group Headquarters
1600 Corporate Landing Pkwy.
Virginia Beach, VA 23454
757-563-1600
www.al-anon.alateen.org

Alcoholics Anonymous
A.A. World Services, Inc., 11th Floor
475 Riverside Dr. at West 120th St.
New York, NY 10115
212-870-3400
www.aa.org

Gamblers Anonymous International Service Office
PO Box 17173
Los Angeles, CA 90017
626-960-3500
www.gamblersanonymous.org

Nar-Anon Family Groups World Service
22527 Crenshaw Blvd., 200B
Torrance, CA 90505
800-477-6271
www.nar-anon.org

Narcotics Anonymous World Services
PO Box 9999
Van Nuys, CA 91409
818-773-9999
www.na.org

Hazelden
PO Box 11
Center City, MN 55012-0011
info@hazelden.org
800-257-7810
24-hour helpline: 800-257-7810
www.hazelden.org

Suggested Reading

Al-Anon Family Group Headquarters, Inc. 1977. *The Dilemma of the Alcoholic Marriage.* New York: Al-Anon.

Conyers, B. 2003. *Addict in the Family: Stories of Loss, Hope, and Recovery.* Center City, MN: Hazelden Publishing.

Steffens, B., and M. Means. 2009. *Your Sexually Addicted Spouse: How Partners Can Cope and Heal*. Far Hills, NJ: New Horizon Press.

Woititz, J. 1986. *Marriage on the Rocks: Learning to Live with Yourself and an Alcoholic*. Deerfield Beach, FL: Health Communications.

Anger, Anxiety, Fear, Grief, and Loneliness

Organizations and Websites

Anxiety Disorders Association of America
8701 Georgia Ave., Ste. 412
Silver Spring, MD 20910
240-485-1001
www.adaa.org

National Anger Management Association
2753 Broadway, Ste. 395
New York, NY 10025
646-485-5116
www.namass.org

National Organization of Parents of Murdered Children
4960 Ridge Ave., Ste. 2
Cincinnati, OH 45209
888-818-7662
www.pomc.org

Suggested Reading

Bourne, E. 2005. *The Anxiety and Phobia Workbook*. 4th ed. Oakland, CA: New Harbinger Publications.

Burns, D. 2007. *When Panic Attacks: The New, Drug-Free Anxiety Therapy That Can Change Your Life*. New York: Three Rivers Press.

Capland, S., and G. Lang. 1995. *Grief's Courageous Journey: A Workbook*. Oakland, CA: New Harbinger Publications.

Davis, M., E. Eshelman, and M. McKay. 2008. *The Relaxation and Stress Reduction Workbook*. 6th ed. Oakland, CA: New Harbinger Publications.

Lerner, Harriet. 2005. *The Dance of Anger*. Danvers, MA: Perennial Currents.

McKay, M., M. Davis, and P. Fanning. 2007. *Thoughts and Feelings: Taking Control of Your Moods and Your Life*. 3rd ed. Oakland, CA: New Harbinger Publications.

McKay, M., and P. Roger. 2000. *The Anger Control Workbook: Simple, Innovative Techniques for Managing Anger and Developing Healthier Ways of Relating*. Oakland, CA: New Harbinger Publications.

Depression and Suicide

Organizations and Websites

American Foundation for Suicide Prevention
120 Wall St., 29th Floor
New York, NY 10005
888-333-AFSP (2377), 212-363-3500
www.afsp.org

Anxiety and Depression Association of America
8701 Georgia Ave., Ste. 412
Silver Spring, MD 20910
240-485-1001
www.adaa.org

Freedom from Fear
718-351-1717, x19
308 Seaview Ave.
Staten Island, NY 10305
www.freedomfromfear.org

National Suicide Prevention Lifeline
800-273-TALK (8255)

The Suicide Prevention Resource Center
43 Foundry Ave.
Waltham, MA 02453-8313
877-GET-SPRC (438-7772)
www.sprc.org

Suggested Reading

Copeland, M. 2001. *The Depression Workbook: A Guide for Living with Depression and Manic Depression.* 2nd ed. Oakland, CA: New Harbinger Publications.

Jamison, K. R. 2000. *Night Falls Fast: Understanding Suicide.* New York: Vintage Books.

Wexler, D. 2006. *Is He Depressed or What? What to Do When the Man You Love Is Irritable, Moody, and Withdrawn.* Oakland, CA: New Harbinger Publications.

Eating and Spending Problems

Organizations and Websites

Debtors Anonymous
General Service Office
PO Box 920888
Needham, MA 02492-0009
800-421-2383
www.debtorsanonymous.org

Overeaters Anonymous, Inc.
6075 Zenith Ct. NE
Rio Rancho, NM 87144-6424
505-891-2664
www.oa.org

Family Violence and Emotional Abuse

Organizations and Websites

American Professional Society on the Abuse of Children
350 Poplar Ave.
Elmhurst, IL 60126
877-402-7722
www.apsac.org

Child Help
National Child Abuse Hotline: 800-4-A-CHILD
800-422-4453
www.childhelp.org

The National Coalition Against Domestic Violence
One Broadway, Ste. B210
Denver, CO 80203
303-839-1852
TTY: 303-839-8459
www.ncadv.org

National Domestic Violence Hotline
800–799–SAFE (7233)
TTY: 800–787–3224
www.thehotline.org

Suggested Reading

Engel, B. 1994. *Encouragements for the Emotionally Abused Woman: Wisdom and Hope.* New York: Ballantine Books.

Jones, A. 2000. *Next Time She'll Be Dead: Battering and How to Stop It.* Boston, MA: Beacon Press.

Kubany, E., M. McCaig, and J. Laconsay. 2004. *Healing the Trauma of Domestic Violence: A Workbook for Women.* Oakland, CA: New Harbinger Publications.

Walker, L. 2009. *The Battered Woman Syndrome.* 3rd ed. New York: Springer Press.

Relationships

Suggested Reading

Gottman, J. 2001. *The Relationship Cure: A Five-Step Guide to Strengthening Your Marriage, Family, and Friendship.* New York: Three Rivers Press.

Gottman, J., and N. Silver. 1999. *The Seven Principles for Making Marriage Work.* New York: Three Rivers Press.

Lerner, H. 2001. *The Dance of Connection: How to Talk To Someone When You're Mad, Hurt, Scared, Frustrated, Insulted, Betrayed, or Desperate.* New York: Harper Collins Publishers.

Matsakis, A. 1998. *Trust After Trauma: A Relationship Guide for Trauma Survivors and Those Who Love Them.* Oakland, CA: New Harbinger Publications.

Phillips, S., and D. Kane. 2009. *Healing Together: A Couple's Guide to Coping with Trauma and PTSD.* Oakland, CA: New Harbinger Publications.

Seligman, M. 2011. *Flourish: A Visionary New Understanding of Happiness and Well-Being.* New York: Free Press.

Heller, L., and A. LaPierre. 2012. *Healing Developmental Trauma: How Early Trauma Affects Self-Regulation, Self-Image, and the Capacity for Relationship.* Berkeley, CA: North Atlantic Books.

Self-Care

Suggested Reading

Albers, S. 2009. *Fifty Ways to Soothe Yourself Without Food*. Oakland, CA: New Harbinger Publications.

Brown, N. 2002. *Whose Life Is It Anyway? When to Stop Taking Care of Their Feelings and Start Taking Care of Your Own*. Oakland, CA: New Harbinger Publications.

Buckingham, M. 2007. *Go Put Your Strengths to Work*. New York: Free Press.

Black. J., and G. Enns. 1998. *Better Boundaries: Owning and Treasuing Your Life*. Oakland, CA: New Harbinger Publications.

Schiraldi, G. 2001. *The Self-Esteem Workbook*. Oakland, CA: New Harbinger Publications.

Nestor, J. 2012. *Nurturing Wellness Through Radical Self-Care: A Living in Balance Guide and Workbook*. Bloomington, IN: Balboa Press.

Sexual Difficulties

Organizations and Websites

American Association of Sexuality Educators, Counselors, and Therapists
1444 I St. NW, Ste. 700
Washington, DC 20005
202-449-1099
www.aasect.org

Sex Addicts Anonymous
PO Box 70949
Houston, TX 77270
800-477-8101
www.saa.org

Suggested Reading

Cervenka, K. 2003. *In the Mood Again: A Couple's Guide to Reawakening Sexual Desire*. Oakland, CA: New Harbinger Publications.

McCarthy, B., and E. McCarthy. 2003. *Rekindling Desire: A Step-by-Step Program to Help Low-Sex and No-Sex Marriages*. New York: Routledge.

Sexual Trauma

Organizations and Websites

National Sexual Assault Hotline
800-656-HOPE

Rape, Abuse, and Incest National Network
2000 L Street NW, Ste. 406
Washington, DC 20036
202-544-1034
www.rainn.org

Suggested Reading

Davis, L. 1990. *The Courage to Heal Workbook: A Guide for Women and Men Survivors of Child Sexual Abuse*. New York: HarperCollins Publishers.

Davis, L. 1991. *Allies in Healing: When the Person You Love Was Sexually Abused as a Child*. New York: HarperCollins Publishers.

Graber, K. 1991. *Ghosts in the Bedroom: A Guide for the Partners of Incest Survivors*. Deerfield Beach, FL: Health Communications.

Matsakis, A. 2003. *The Rape Recovery Handbook: Step-by-Step Help for Survivors of Sexual Trauma*. Oakland, CA: New Harbinger Publications.

Trauma and Trauma Recovery

Organizations and Websites

American Psychiatric Association
1000 Wilson Blvd., Suite 1825
Arlington, VA 22209
888-35-PSYCH (77924)
www.psych.org

American Psychological Association
750 First St. NE
Washington, DC 20002-4242
800-374-2721; 202-336-5500
www.apa.org

Gift from Within: An International Nonprofit Organization for
Survivors of Trauma and Victimization
16 Cobb Hill Rd.
Camden, ME 04843
207-236-8858
www.giftfromwithin.org

International Society for Traumatic Stress Studies
111 Deer Lake Rd., Ste. 100
Deerfield, IL 60015
847-480-9028
www.istss.org

National Center for PTSD: US Department of Veterans Affairs
810 Vermont Ave. NW
Washington, DC 20420
www.ptsd.va.gov

National Association of Social Workers
750 First St. NE, Ste. 700
Washington, DC 20002-4241
202-408-8600
www.socialworkers.org

Suggested Reading

Alley, L., and W. Stevenson. *Back from War: A Quest for Life After Death*. Midlothian, VA: Exceptional Publishing.

Armstrong, K., S. Best, and P. Domenici. 2005. *Courage After Fire: Coping Strategies for Troops Returning from Iraq and Afghanistan and Their Families*. Berkeley, CA: Ulysses Press.

Firdman, M., and L. Stone. 2008. *After the War Zone: A Practical Guide for Returning Troops and Their Families.* Philadelphia, PA: De Capo Press.

Hoge, C. 2012. *Once a Warrior—Always a Warrior: Navigating the Transition from Combat to Home—Including Combat Stress, PTSD, and mTBI.* 1st ed. Guilford, CT: Globe Pequot Press.

Mason, P. 2009. *Recovering from the War: A Guide for All Veterans, Family Members, Friends, and Therapists.* High Springs, FL: Patience Press.

Matsakis, A. 1996. *I Can't Get Over It: A Handbook for Trauma Survivors.* 2nd ed. Oakland, CA: New Harbinger Publications.

Matsakis, A. 2007. *Back from the Front: Combat Stress and the Family.* Baltimore, MD: The Sidran Foundation.

Raja, S. 2013. *Overcoming Trauma and PTSD: A Workbook Integrating Skills from ACT, DBT, and CBT.* Oakland, CA: New Harbinger Publications.

Regel, S., and S. Joseph. 2010. *The Facts: Post-Traumatic Stress.* Oxford, UK: Oxford University Press.

Roukema, R. 2003. *What Every Patient, Family, Friend, and Caregiver Needs to Know About Psychiatry.* 2nd ed. Arlington, VA: American Psychiatric Publishing.

Shapiro, Robin. 2010. *The Trauma Treatment Handbook: Protocols Across the Spectrum.* New York: W. W. Norton.

Williams, M., and S. Poijula. 2002. *The PTSD Workbook: Simple, Effective Techniques for Overcoming Traumatic Stress Symptoms.* Oakland, CA: New Harbinger Publications.

Wood, J., and M. Wood. 2008. *Therapy 101: A Brief Look at Modern Psychotherapy Techniques and How They Can Help*. Oakland, CA: New Harbinger Publications.

Finding a Therapist

To find a therapist, get recommendations from doctors; hospitals; friends and acquaintances; local mental health and social services agencies; and local or state chapters of the International Society for Traumatic Stress Studies, the American Psychiatric Association, the American Psychological Association, the American Association for Marriage and Family Therapy, or the National Association of Social Workers.

If your partner is a veteran, contact the nearest Department of Veterans Affairs Medical Center (www.va.gov). If he's active duty, contact the family services, social services, or mental health unit of any US Army (www.army.mil), US Navy (www.navy.com), US Air Force (www.airforce.com), or US Marine Corps (www.marines.com) facility, or check their websites for information about services for military staff and veterans and their partners and families. Look for information on support groups; individual, couples, and family counseling; and financial and other support services.

Contact information for all of the above organizations can be found in the phone directory, online, at your local library, or at local mental health or social service organizations.

Be sure to ask for a therapist or program specializing in PTSD and any other problems your partner is experiencing. In seeking a therapist for yourself, it's also best if the therapist has specialized knowledge of PTSD. Otherwise your life situation may not be well understood.

References

American Psychiatric Association. 2013. *Diagnostic and Statistical Manual of Mental Disorders.* 5th ed. Washington, DC: American Psychiatric Association.

Berman, A. and M. Pompili, eds. 2011. *Medical Conditions Associated with Suicide Risk.* Washington, DC: American Association of Suicidology.

Burns, D. 2007. *When Panic Attacks: The New, Drug-Free Anxiety Therapy That Can Change Your Life.* New York: Three Rivers Press.

Dedert, E. A., M. E. Becker, B. F. Fuemeler, L. E. Braxton, P. S. Calhoun, and J. C. Beckham. 2010. "Childhood Traumatic Stress and Obesity in Women: The Intervening Effects of PTSD and MDD. *Journal of Traumatic Stress.* 23: 785–93.

Duff, K. 1993. *The Alchemy of Illness.* New York: Bell Tower.

Fisher, B., P. Giblin, and M. Hoopes. 1982. "Healthy Family Functioning: What Therapists Say and What Families Want." *Journal of Marital and Family Therapy.* 8: 273–85.

Gottman, J., and N. Silver. 1999. *The Seven Principles for Making Marriage Work*. New York: Three Rivers Press.

Gradus, J. 2011. "Epidemiology of PTSD." National Center for PTSD, United States Department of Veterans Affairs. http://www.ptsd.va.gov/professional/pages/epidemiological -facts-ptsd.asp.

Guerney, B., Jr. 1987. *Relationship Enhancement: Marital/Family Therapist's Manual*. 2nd ed. State College, PA: Ideals, Inc.

Haley, S. 1974. "When the Patient Reports Atrocities. *Archives of General Psychiatry*. 30: 191–94.

Herodotus. 1890. *The History of Herodotus*. Translated by G. Macaulay. London: Macmillan.

Jay, J. 2001. "Terrible Knowledge." *Family Therapist Networker*, November/December, 18–29.

Johnson, S. 2002. *Emotionally Focused Couples Therapy for Trauma Survivors*. New York: The Guilford Press.

Joseph, S. 2011. *What Doesn't Kill Us: The New Psychology of Post-traumatic Growth*. New York: Basic Books.

Klott, J. 2012. *Suicide and Psychological Pain: Prevention That Works*. Eau Clair, WI: Premier Publishing and Media.

Kubany, E., and F. Manke. 1995. "Cognitive Therapy for Trauma-Related Guilt: Conceptual Bases and Treatment Outlines." *Cognitive and Behavioral Practice*. 2: 27–62.

Matsakis, A. 2002. *Rape Recovery: A Handbook for Survivors*. Oakland, CA: New Harbinger Publications.

———. 2007. *Back from the Front: Combat Stress and the Family*. Baltimore, MD: The Sidran Foundation.

May, R. 1994. *The Courage to Create*. New York: W. W. Norton.

Milam, J., and K. Ketchan. 1981. *Under the Influence: A Guide to the Myths and Realities of Alcoholism*. NY: Bantam Books.

Morrison, J. 1997. *When Psychological Problems Mask Medical Disorders: A Guide for Psychotherapists*. New York: The Guilford Press.

Nazarian, D., R. Kimerling, and S. Frayne. 2012. "Posttraumatic Stress Disorder, Substance Use Disorders, and Medical Comorbidity Among U.S. Veterans." *Journal of Traumatic Stress.* 25: 220–25.

Ortlepp, K., and M. Friedman. 2002. "Prevalence and Correlates of Secondary Traumatic Stress in Workplace Lay Trauma Counselors." *Journal of Traumatic Stress.* 15: 213–22.

Quittner, A., and R. Schultz, eds. 1998. "Caregiving for Children and Adults with Chronic Conditions: A Life Span Approach." *Health Psychology.* 17: 2.

Regel, S., and S. Joseph. 2010. *The Facts: Post-Traumatic Stress*. Oxford, UK: Oxford University Press.

Seligman, M. 2011. *Flourish: A Visionary New Understanding of Happiness and Well-Being*. New York: Free Press.

Seng, J., M. Clark, A. McCarthy, and D. Ronis. 2006. "PTSD and Physical Comorbidity Among Women Receiving Medicaid: Receiving Service-Use Data." *Journal of Traumatic Stress.* 19: 45–56.

Shepard, B. 2003. *A War of Nerves: Soldiers and Psychiatrists in the Twentieth Century*. Cambridge, MA: Harvard University Press.

Stein, D. 2004. *Clinical Manual of Anxiety Disorders*. Alexandria, VA: American Psychiatric Association.

van der Kolk, B., A. McFarlane, and L. Weisaeth, eds. 1996. *Traumatic Stress: The Effects of Overwhelming Experience on Mind, Body, and Society*. New York: Guilford Press.

Walker, L. 2009. *The Battered Woman Syndrome*. 3rd ed. New York: Springer Publishing.

Weber, T. 2010. *Hitler's First War: Adolph Hitler, the Men of the List Regiment, and the First World War*. New York: Oxford University Press.

Aphrodite T. Matsakis, PhD, is an internationally recognized expert in trauma and the author of several books dealing with traumatic reactions, including *I Can't Get Over It!*, *Trust After Trauma*, *The Rape Recovery Handbook,* and *Vietnam Wives: Women and Children Facing the Challenge of Living with Veterans with Post-Traumatic Stress Disorder.* Matsakis has over thirty-five years of experience working with veterans, abused persons, and other trauma survivors; has taught at several major universities; and has conducted dozens of seminars for trauma survivors and trauma therapists.

FROM OUR PUBLISHER—

As the publisher at New Harbinger and a clinical psychologist since 1978, I know that emotional problems are best helped with evidence-based therapies. These are the treatments derived from scientific research (randomized controlled trials) that show what works. Whether these treatments are delivered by trained clinicians or found in a self-help book, they are designed to provide you with proven strategies to overcome your problem.

Therapies that aren't evidence-based—whether offered by clinicians or in books—are much less likely to help. In fact, therapies that aren't guided by science may not help you at all. That's why this New Harbinger book is based on scientific evidence that the treatment can relieve emotional pain.

This is important: if this book isn't enough, and you need the help of a skilled therapist, use the following resources to find a clinician trained in the evidence-based protocols appropriate for your problem. And if you need more support—a community that understands what you're going through and can show you ways to cope—resources for that are provided below, as well.

Real help is available for the problems you have been struggling with. The skills you can learn from evidence-based therapies will change your life.

Matthew McKay, PhD
Publisher, New Harbinger Publications

new harbinger
CELEBRATING
40 YEARS

**If you need a therapist, the following organization
can help you find a therapist trained in cognitive behavioral therapy (CBT).**

The Association for Behavioral & Cognitive Therapies (ABCT) Find-a-Therapist service offers a list of therapists schooled in CBT techniques. Therapists listed are licensed professionals who have met the membership requirements of ABCT and who have chosen to appear in the directory.

Please visit www.abct.org and click on *Find a Therapist*.

**For additional support for patients, family, and friends,
please contact the following:**

National Center for PTSD
Visit www.ptsd.va.gov

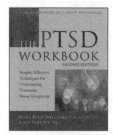

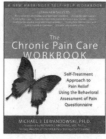